THE
COURAGE
TO LIVE A
MEANINGFUL
LIFE

THE
COURAGE
TO LIVE A
MEANINGFUL
LIFE

A JOURNEY OF TRUTH,
FORGIVENESS, AND POSITIVITY

ANDY BUI

ISBN Paperback: 979-8-218-41876-2
ISBN Hardcover: 979-8-9917372-1-0
ISBN Ebook: 979-8-9917372-0-3

Interior Design: Creative Publishing Book Design

www.andybui.life

*To my wife – To bring light to you, to bring life to me.
To my boys, Max and Micah – May this unlock
your minds to their full potential. Unlimited
possibilities are within your reach.*

CONTENTS

CONTENTS

INTRODUCTION

STARING THROUGH THE TINY airplane window, everything looked insignificant. With vague memories of my childhood in Vietnam, I touched American soil for the first time in 1986 at the age of five. Raised in a Buddhist home as a Christian, my apathy toward religion was apparent, and I had avoided the conversation about it throughout life. I was quite confused, as I grew up without a concrete belief system. My father, who I do not recall in detail, is Catholic, while my mother is Buddhist. My mother converted to marry my father, who already had three daughters—and desired a son.

The post-Vietnam War era was chaotic in my homeland. My mother opposed having another child, and her three children were all older. With faith, she gave my father a son. The opportunity of a lifetime presented itself; my mother decided to leave my father to pursue a better life for us. She took only three of her children—Lynn, Nina,

1

and me—and fled to America. We were forced to leave my half-brother, Tung, behind due to missing documentation and a limited immigration window. My mother carries that burden to this day.

Despite empty pockets and no concrete plans, we were relieved to have escaped a country of communism and tyranny. My father died of a heart attack in Vietnam when I was a freshman in high school. The sorrow, grief, and self-pity have been embedded in me throughout my adulthood.

As an above-average college student with only one year of school left, my motivation and determination took a back seat to the heartbreak of my first love. Young and experiencing these feelings for the first time, I failed in the footsteps of hurt and anger. As I tried to cope and deal with the emotions, my carefree lifestyle led to a litany of problems in my life.

This book is essentially one long confession to my family, the world, God, and myself. It symbolizes the courage to live a meaningful life, overcome negative experiences, and prevail for a greater cause. That courage manifested the idea to write this memoir and to improve for God, be obedient, and carry out His plan.

Although we may think our insignificant individual lives have minimal impact on the world, each of us contributes to and impacts humanity more than we know—one story at a time. More positive, life-changing stories should be heard. Hopefully, one day, they will outweigh the negative ones that have shaped our lives.

This book shares the positive and negative experiences of my sudden life transformation. From journaling in a note application on my phone to what is now this book, *The Courage to Live a Meaningful Life*, the initial intent was to improve. Now the purpose is to share that, through faith, we can give meaning to living well for others, the youth, in particular.

The first few chapters of this book document my various struggles and addictions. The remainder of the book consists of the stream-of-consciousness-style thoughts and interpretations I had during my recovery, stemming from my experiences with faith. While I turn my life around and become a new man, I share my newly acquired perspectives.

I am grateful for my second life, and equally grateful for my family and friends. May these words encourage, give hope, and find a place in your heart to live meaningfully.

Many people know the saying "You can't change overnight." While it is true that change often requires time and effort, one can change overnight. Sudden transformations are possible, albeit challenging.

For many years, I was adamant that the purpose of life was centered around family, friends, and career. It is not. My purpose is to pursue an everlasting relationship with

God. I now know my genuine destiny is to seek and follow faith through Christ. I trust that He will care for all of his children, including me, and lead with wisdom and words to share on this endless journey.

CHAPTER ONE

PATH TO SIN

OVERCOMING THE FEAR OF CONFESSION

"LET'S GO TO CHURCH," I told my wife.

We arrived at Word of Life, a nondenominational church, on Easter Sunday of 2023. We had not attended church in years. Living just five minutes away, this would be my first time there. I have lived in Brandon, Mississippi, for twenty years, and my wife has always told me we must attend Word of Life one day, as I drive past it daily on my commute to work.

Finally, we entered this new world. An aura of negative energy followed as I walked into the church, thinking to myself, This is like a concert. The interior was huge, with a big stage and hundreds of people in attendance. My first impression of Pastor Joel was negative. He looked short, wore glasses and outdated casual clothing, and was balding. I was turned off; the evil spirit had influenced me.

While he spoke in a high-pitched voice, something spiritual happened to me. There was a deep connection to every word preached. He spoke clearly, with passion and heart. I was most captivated by his story of how he almost walked away from faith after the passing of his father. This was his reason for postponing the construction of the church, as it had been unfinished for years. The message was heard. The words no longer sounded like syllables bouncing off my ears. I was mesmerized.

But seeing one of my neighbors who attended the service, my negativity returned. She was on her phone.

Why are you on your phone? I wondered. Why are you here if you are not listening to the message? Later, it dawned on me that she was taking notes.

I left the sermon with great clarity, understanding, and hope—revived with a glimpse of purpose and fulfillment. It was a profound experience that ended with an excellent discussion with my wife over lunch on a warm, clear day.

The revelation could have happened anytime, anywhere, with anyone. But it happened that day in the moments after Pastor Joel uttered his fruitful words; I had already accepted Christ and faith—a realization that would stay with me. My guilt had opened the gates to allow the acceptance of the church.

Soon after the service, a voice rang out, clear and specific. However, I was unable to identify it at the time. It was either God or my wife's deceased mother, who I had been praying to. But those prayers had been tarnished by my cries for help and false intent, and induced with negative energy.

The voice told me, "You must confess to your wife. You must tell her all your darkest secrets and sins." It told me not to confess to a priest or anyone else. I was terrified that the suggestion would cost me my wife, children, and life.

While under the influence of marijuana at night to help me sleep, another voice filtered through. This one was different; it had a soft, devious, persuasive tone. It had evil intentions.

"You do not need to confess. She does not know your dark secrets; no one does. It has been seventeen years. Why risk ruining your life?"

Morning came, and the voice of God returned, telling me to confess and speak my truth. After battling with the two voices for months, I finally found the strength and courage to tell my wife everything.

APATHY TOWARD RELIGION

Am I Buddhist or Catholic? I distinctly remember asking myself this in high school. At that time, growing into manhood, I was debating if I should be like my mother and the rest of my family and become Buddhist or follow my late father's religion as I was baptized. I wanted to be considerate and respectful of others and other religions when I decided which path to take.

I went to the temples, where the Buddhists held their functions and festivals, with my older sister, Nina. Chinese New Year at the temples was my favorite, as they had food, fireworks, and the "Dragon Dance" (traditional Chinese dance in costume). The first time I remember going to church was with my mother's boyfriend, Frank, who was Mexican. Frank, who I call Franko, and his family welcomed my mother and me into their Christian-based family. I call them my second family.

Karen, Franko's oldest daughter, had an older daughter and a son one year younger than me, with whom I would spend most of my summers. As my relationship with them grew, my visits and encounters with the church became frequent, as both kids attended a private Christian school. The person I looked up to the most, besides Franko, was his youngest son, Kiki. He was full of life, a man of faith, with a beautiful wife and a young daughter who was around my age and a successful landscaping business. His role and interactions with his family were what I wanted when I had my own family. I would stay with him on the weekends and go to church. His family wore fresh, ironed clothing, and I was surprised and impressed, as I had never seen my family iron anything.

My mother later moved to Mississippi to help my oldest sister, Lynn, with her children. I stayed with Franko for a few more years and then moved back in with my family as I entered high school.

"Andy, what is that you're wearing on your neck?" a high school counselor asked me.

"It's a Buddha made of jade," I responded.

"That's nice, but you should wear a cross," she continued. She proceeded to tell me a story about how she was in an accident, and without Christ she would not have survived.

I overlooked the heartfelt content of the story and focused only on why she rejected my Buddha and its religion. There are also incredible stories of Buddha helping people, especially in my homeland, Vietnam. I was taken aback by the fact that she was inconsiderate of other people's religions, even though she was a sweet, loving counselor. Her approach was gentle, but it felt forced. I thought about coming up with a false story about Buddhism, that it had saved my sister's life and she turned to Buddha, too. But that would have done me no good. I was young and wanted to retaliate, but that meant I would be doing the same thing she was doing. I did not want to force any religion on anyone.

Is this what religion is about? I wondered. Who is right and who is wrong? Both religions have similar life values and morals. The difference is that one worships one God and the other multiple Gods, and the rituals differ. I wore the jade necklace simply because I liked how it looked. My mother gave it to me, along with another necklace featuring a cross, as she respected both Buddhism and Christianity.

After my conversation with the counselor, I gained clarity and resolved my inner conflict. I had no desire to be a part of either religion. The unfavorable exchange led me to not have an interest in faith. The displacement toward all religions had set its course.

THE HEARTBREAK

After completing two years of community college, I met a girl on AOL during the rise of the internet. Our relationship became my first serious love, inspiring me to attend a graphic design school in Phoenix, where she lived. Well into the fourth year of our relationship, I was in the last year of obtaining a visual communications degree. We began to spend a lot of time with two newly acquainted friends; though they were not a couple, we hung out as couples. Months flew by, and the two friends, my girlfriend, and I, were inseparable.

With complete trust in my girlfriend and new friend, I was unaware of the development of their relationship. I was in school and had a part-time job as a nail technician. He went to college and did not work, and my girlfriend was not working then. Their schedules aligned, and they spent the daytime together.

One night, my girlfriend did not come home and said she spent the night at her girlfriend's place, raising my suspicion. Interestingly, my guy friend was also unavailable that night. I called her girlfriend, who she said she spent the night with, and pleaded for her honesty. It took a while, but she finally gave in and told me the truth.

"She did not stay with me last night, Andy."

After uncovering the affair, I asked my girlfriend and friend for a meeting. They confessed that they had feelings for each other and, indeed, spent the night together.

"If he can treat you better than me, then choose him, but know that I love you," I told her at the end of the meeting. Then I calmly walked to where I had placed a small Miracle Blade steak knife. Premeditated, and with force, I attempted to stab my right torso. Silence filled the room. The cowardly plan may not have been to take my life in front of them, but to regain her attention. I wore two white shirts that day, one of which was thick—the impact did puncture through and bled.

SINNING CAME EASY

After discovering the betrayal of my girlfriend and friend, I felt only hate and pain; nothing seemed to matter. I did not care about anything and was fearless with my choices and behavior. After the heartbreak, I met new friends, and a carefree lifestyle began. I experimented with what the other side of life had to offer: influences of the evil spirit. Drugs surfaced, and, with ease, marijuana, ecstasy, and cocaine were within reach. Most drugs were sampled, with the exception of heroin. Ecstasy was the favored choice, as it was at its peak during the early 2000s. The colored pills were everywhere at parties and raves. Going out almost every night, I began to lose control of myself.

My school was only blocks away from Arizona State University, the number three-ranked party college in the nation. One of my roommates was in a fraternity, which boosted the partying. While he could still balance and maintain his schooling, I could not.

One of my friends suggested, "Let's go to Vegas. It's only four hours away."

"I'm down," I said without hesitation.

College parties, especially at a large university, were great, but Las Vegas was a whole different animal. Flushed with excitement, we experienced an unforgettable feeling every time we crossed the mountaintop, and the neon city lit up the sky. It seemed like no one ever slept in "Sin City." (I now feel indifferent to the phrase "What happens in Vegas, stays in Vegas.")

To fill the void and pain left by my previous relationship, I jumped right into another one in Vegas. Weekend trips to the city began affecting my part-time job as a nail technician—my character and work ethic declined, as I hopped from one salon to another. I tried freelancing my graphic design skills, but had no luck. Desperate, gambling became a way for me to try to make money.

"Fantasy draft? What's that?" I asked one of my roommates, when he mentioned "the draft date."

I was intrigued, although I was not into football at the time. But once I learned money was involved, it did not take me long to become interested in the hobby.

"The Asian gambling blood." This phrase had surrounded my life. Growing up in a family with a gambling history, I knew what it meant. With casinos within close driving distance of where I lived in Tempe, Arizona, quick money became the focus, as greed was born with brute strength. Having a new love interest in Vegas, and going to school, money was needed. Living independently for the first time, I failed to be disciplined with my finances.

During a month-long stint in Vegas, I pawned every possession, including a laptop and car. Trying to gamble my way back to Phoenix and school, I realized this was not for me. Trust, honor, and dignity deserted me. Lies filled my soul. I became a burden to my family. I needed help and I needed to go home.

LIFE RESULTING FROM DEATH

After a carefree phase in Phoenix and Las Vegas, I broke up with my Vegas girlfriend and dropped out of school with one semester left, as I was already on academic probation. I moved back to Mississippi and stayed with my sister Lynn.

Trying to find my way back and adapt to the South's slow pace, I spent time with my nephew and nieces. I ran into an ex while taking the kids to a go-cart park.

"Come out tonight with us," she said enthusiastically. "There's a Chinese girl who just moved into town from Mississippi State University. You should meet her."

"I'll see you tonight!" I said. That night, I met the woman who would become my wife.

My two friends and I met up with my ex and her friends at a nightclub in Jackson. An old car dealership that had been turned into a large venue, it was popular at the time and played a mixture of hip-hop and dance music.

She was stunningly youthful with small features like a Chinese porcelain doll, dark hair with blonde highlights, and a fashionable sense. However, her main attraction was her sociability, which outshined even her petite frame. She stood slightly above my shoulders, even in heels. She was four-foot-eight, and I was barely five-foot-five; I had the rare sensation of feeling tall, which gave me a sense of confidence. Growing up watching Chinese movies, I always wanted to date a Chinese girl. But these initial thoughts were brief, and meeting my future wife was not love at first sight; it was more like meeting an acquaintance.

After our introduction that night, I had to fly back to Phoenix and gather my things to move to Mississippi. We connected and met up three months later, and my best friend came with me. At that time, he and I were both single.

"You talk to her first," my buddy told me.

"I just got out of a relationship. You talk to her," I insisted.

She and my best friend exchanged phone numbers, and he ended up talking to her first. About two weeks went by, and there was only casual conversation between the two of them.

"Have you taken her on a date yet?" I asked my buddy.

"Not yet," he replied.

"I heard that her sister is moving to town. Since nothing is developing between you two, we can switch. I can talk to her, and you can talk to her little sister." He happily agreed, and our guy talk ended with a plan. I wasted no time asking her out—and the rest is history.

After five years of dating, my girlfriend and I got married on September 18, 2011. I pressed for a big wedding, which would be my first, but she was not keen on the idea. Nonetheless, I spent thousands of dollars on the wedding to display my status to family and friends. Two years passed, and talks of children began.

"You two need to have a baby now," my wife's mother demanded, after informing us that she was diagnosed with cancer.

I could sense the stress, worry, and sadness as my pregnant wife cared for her sick mother. Throughout the following year, my wife never complained during the whole pregnancy, while she drove a total of eight hours round-trip to take her mother for treatments. I had a newfound appreciation for my wife.

On a serene Monday morning, at 9:02, my beloved mother-in-law peacefully departed from this world. Two days later, at 9:01 a.m., my firstborn, Max, inhaled his first pure breath on Earth.

According to Asian tradition and culture, it was customary for us not to attend the funeral, as my wife had just given birth. But she refused to abide by this rule. We had to delay our departure from the hospital, as we waited for Max to recover from jaundice. When he was discharged five days later, we went straight from the hospital to the funeral.

CHAPTER TWO

WORSHIPPING MYSELF

PRIDE: NOT A GOOD THING?

A NEW CHAPTER IN MY life had begun. I had found the ideal wife, had the big wedding I had always wanted, and started a family. When an opportunity to build a new house and obtain ownership of a small salon came around, I felt like I had made it. They say your marriage will last if you can survive building a home together—this was accomplished. My goals and desires were achieved as planned, and I was proud of myself for my life, despite the bad choices I had made. Pride had found a home and fully furnished it. I always thought having pride was a good trait.

The salon steadily increased its revenue. However, I became excessively proud and considered myself superior as the teacher, not the student. I was unwilling to take direction from anyone beneath me; no one could tell me what to do.

The idea and influence of a family helped control my gambling addiction. Somewhat contained, casino gambling and football betting ceded to fantasy football. It helped me enjoy the habit while the financial risks were manageable. I thought the gambling problem had been overcome until the habit, again, became uncontrollable with an enormous amount of fantasy leagues. Addictions slowly crawled back, cloaked in other forms.

MY BIGGEST SECRET

My pornography addiction was my biggest secret. My consumption of pornography only added to the objectification of women. The fascination started when I was around twelve years old and accidentally came across the Playboy channel when home alone. The infamous, illegal "black box" was in many homes, including ours. Anytime the house was empty, and I had a chance, the television went straight to that channel.

This led to more severe behavior as puberty began. Watching pornography became a daily routine. Throughout high school and college, thoughts of lust and imagery took over my mind. Even when in a physical relationship with another human, it did not outweigh the pleasures of harsh, hardcore pornography. Fantasizing about having multiple partners and different sex acts was a joyful sin. In a way, the addiction helped me be faithful in my relationships. Hiding this shameful addiction was a far better option than seeking the pleasures of another lover. In reality, I was still cheating and dishonest, but it felt like a lesser offense.

Like an incurable, prolonged disease, the addiction followed me into my marriage. It had become manageable and less aggressive, though. The thoughts developed automatically whenever free time presented itself. The anticipation grew stronger and stronger over the years. Though there were attempts to resist and fight back the urge in the beginning years of my marriage, I ultimately gave up and gave in.

I was paralyzed by my most shameful vice almost my entire life. Consumed and obsessed, I hid the addiction from my wife, family, and friends. As much as I had expressed repugnancy to pornography, the thoughts of my family finding out would ruin this mirage—desecrate my existence. Each day, the lies became more complicated.

Pornography was growing in popularity in the mainstream media; the industry had become openly talked about. And it was becoming a bigger part of my life, too. With this influence, the sinful pleasure became part of me.

LOSING MYSELF TO SUBSTANCE ABUSE

After my second knee surgery, I sought painkillers, as I was in my early thirties and experiencing a lot of discomfort. The usage gradually increased when I acquired the salon, which was the primary source funding the habit. My addiction to painkillers was unbearable at times. Constant thoughts of the drug became more frequent throughout the day. Spending thousands of dollars per month and consuming eight to twelve pills per day was the norm. It had taken over my mind and life, but this was not the breaking point.

I was going into debt, as I neglected to pay my bills. My body craved the white, oval-shaped pills, and my mind was fixated only on the steady flow of the supply. I suddenly and unexpectedly started falling asleep multiple times throughout the day, whether at work, home, or driving. I constantly checked the time. At the peak of my addiction, two pills lasted only two to three hours. When the feeling slowly began to fade, nothing else seemed to matter other than sustaining the high.

It was not until Max was around two years old that I was concerned or admitted to myself that I had an addiction. My son had become my life, and the hard reality that I may one day not be there for him, because of my selfish needs, devastated me. One random, blissful day, the abundant life in my son's big, bright, almond-shaped, brown eyes finally outweighed the formidable pills. I was adamant that I was not going to fail him.

Thanksgiving was on the horizon, and I planned to use the break to kick the habit, knowing the recovery would take more than a week. I pushed to take a family trip to Greenville, Mississippi, to spend the holiday with my wife's father, to try to hide my shame. I secluded myself in a room away from my son, wife, and father-in-law. Scared of losing my wife and son, I disguised my withdrawal as a sickness.

The pain slowly eased its way in—the withdrawal left me in agony for about ten days. It felt like I was isolated in the darkest depths of the ocean. The first three days were dim and, by far, the worst feeling I had ever endured, though I happened to catch a small glimmer of hope one night in Greenville—a distant star isolated in the night sky. Constantly fighting the misery with thoughts of Max, I was determined to conquer this demon.

Feeling alone, I sought company through online interactions and powerful stories of how many others overcame their addictions. Their uplifting stories were a testament to the power of will and hope, demonstrating that it is indeed possible to break free from the grip of addiction. The support of online communities was one of the primary reasons I was able to overcome my opioid use. After successfully conquering the addiction, I headed back to the blogs and online communities to share my success stories, to help, support, and give hope as they have helped me.

Defeating the opioid addiction was an accomplishment; however, it also added to my inflated sense of self-pride. My spirit was still without purpose, still damaged and lost. The addictions had brought a sense of shame to my soul and psyche.

THE SMELL

One day, Max, who is ten now, said to me, "Dad, please stop smoking." Although Max did not know what I was smoking, the marijuana smell was potent, as the smell followed me from the yard into the house.

I paused and was quite surprised. Unfortunately, that did not deter me from smoking marijuana. My wife does not mind me smoking it, but hates the smell.

Smoking marijuana gave me a different sense of falseness and doubt. It was more of a feeling than a voice telling me that the path I have been on was based on false hope. The high was met with doubt. I was terrified. I did not desire that feeling, and experienced it only when I was high. The fake, gratifying feeling became meaningless, and I had identified the evil intent behind smoking.

I decided to quit smoking to set a positive example for my son and lead him away from the path of addiction. To guide and teach him self-control. I felt alive again when I was sober—bursting with positive energy. The genuine positive feeling finally outweighed the artificial sensation.

On the second day of being sober, I lay in bed at midnight, unable to sleep. Looking around and seeing everyone asleep, I thought of heading to the back porch for a marijuana fix. No one will know, I thought. No one will smell it. But I shook the

25

deceitful thoughts and began to think positively. Be truthful, be better, be a good person, and overcome this addiction.

On the third day of sobriety, Max woke me early with a hug and kiss. I told him, "Hey, Max, Daddy hasn't smoked in three days."

He replied, "I'm so proud of you, Daddy!" And he hugged and kissed me.

That brought me to tears; it broke my heart and pieced it back together simultaneously. I never wanted to experience that feeling of doubt and disappointment from him ever again. Smoking had finally lost its value. Not only was it damaging my mental state, but it crippled me physically.

I now realize I have gone through distinct phases of addiction throughout my life. Indulging in food developed into an addiction. Late-night snacks became routine, as I thought they might ease my pain and suffering. Trying to cover, hide, and forget the stress and depression with the cravings, I began to gain weight.

THE SELF-INDULGING ADDICTIONS

My thoughts about my addictions were that I was morally flawed and lacked willpower. Facing these addictive, self-imploding behaviors has led me to research and explore the scientific aspects of addiction and their relationship to spirituality. This general information coincides with stories that have led me to conclude that individuals with a stronger spirit are more likely to identify and overcome these behaviors. It is ultimately a choice; the science of our genetic makeup does not bind us.

As I collect more information and synthesize from multiple sources and my own spiritual experience, I realize we have a biological tendency to evade accountability and the consequences of our choices—the inherent tendency of our minds to shift the result of our choices to a medical condition. This excuse prolongs the disorder.

Addiction can cause changes in brain chemistry, as it is a chronic disease. It can take many different forms, but two of the most common are substance and behavioral addictions. Both stimulate and activate our brain's reward system. We are biologically driven to pursue rewards, causing our bodies to release dopamine, which produces feelings of pleasure. Addiction trains our brain to repeat the behavior and crave more.

Even though, in most cases, addictions begin with decisions, it is not simply a matter of behavior or willpower. It is also influenced by biology and can stem from a weakened mind. Our minds and bodies are interconnected.

At the root of every addiction lies the presence of pain. We go through phases in our lives, and when we experience an adverse event or situation, our minds can be weakened and consumed by feelings of pain, anger, worry, suffering, and stress. We all look for pleasure or something that can ease and suppress our pain. The negative energy associated with stress and change can sometimes develop into an addiction. The energy changes how the brain works and can become a disorder.

Instead of having the courage to confront the source of our pain and focus on the things we desire most, we tend to seek external sources to help cope and distract us, such as food, alcohol, drugs, spending money, and social media. Over time, this can become a habit, and we become addicted to the behavior or feeling the relevant action brings. It is not about the vices themselves but allowing those vices to control our lives. However, these are short-term solutions that can lead us to become long-term prisoners of the vices—our minds become handcuffed. It only reinforces our addiction and makes it stronger.

Sometimes we overlook certain behavioral and substance addictions. Some addictions are considered high risk, and we understand their destruction, while others are deemed minor risks, and we may ignore the warnings, thus devaluing the addiction. However, even lesser types of vices contribute to the loss of self-control, making us more susceptible to other addictions.

To take charge of our lives, we need to be confident in our choices and not let our vices control us. Break the habits that may develop into characteristics of addiction. We must strive to identify and separate ourselves from any addiction. We must know our family history, manage our stress by strengthening our minds, and avoid or limit non-medical substances.

A healthy flow of energy and a positive mind can manifest happiness, love, and positivity while defending the penetration of negativity during challenging times. Practicing positive thinking, forgiveness, and love daily is important to nourish the mind with positivity. This will reawaken and help with addiction when moments of weakness arise. A strong mind will result in more vital discipline and routine and a healthier, happier lifestyle.

External substances can change and rewire the brain's structure. The inner spirit can also change our brain. Addiction leads to self-destruction, which eventually leads to death. Be more than ourselves. Be more than our desires.

CHAPTER THREE

THE SUDDEN JOURNEY

WELCOMING DARKNESS

*"Our true moral character is shown
when we face adversity."*

LYING IN BED, SOAKED in stress and worry, I stared hopelessly at my two angelic boys, who were sound asleep next to me. This time, however, it felt different. A waterfall of hopeful thoughts began to rush through: They deserve better than this negative energy; they deserve a better life. They can achieve unimaginable possibilities, and I needed to be their guide and set an example. Learning of the reckless decisions in my past had overburdened my family, and I had more to lose than just myself.

Before I found faith and confessed at the beginning of 2023, my small nail salon business faced unforeseen adversity and was forced to shut down for five months due to contractual lease disputes. Three months prior, we were struck with the news of relocating the company, which added stress as we approached the holiday season. The fear of losing the business and my family left me drained and lifeless.

Depressed, I became fixated on negative energy, and the financial hardship of losing substantially in stocks due to the struggling markets after the pandemic only added to the stress and depression. I felt haunted by failures of every kind and was on the brink of losing everything. Depleted with the feeling that there was no way out and surrendering to life itself, I began to search for self-help and spiritual videos.

Responding every day with aggression, I was mean and distant. I frequently yelled at the children, thinking it was the only way of disciplining them. As a nail technician, I dreaded doing my wife's nails. I could never satisfy her. I hated going to work with no desire to be social. Though forced to be friendly, the simple energy needed to greet the clients with a smile was not present. Struggling to hide the hollowness—the silhouette of a slow, soulless zombie was prominent. I was miserable.

The back porch, where I smoked for hours, was my domain. I binge-watched shows, movies, and TV series in my bedroom to help distract myself. Meaningless interactions on social media consumed most of my time, while I concerned myself with politics and news that were beyond my control.

Further feeding the negativity and mentally exhausted, I was helpless to cure and improve my life. I had failed, specifically in providing for my family. The feeling of defeat and inability to provide for the two boys hit hard. How can I teach them to succeed in life if I am unsuccessful?

I had lied every day to be perceived as this well-put-together, confident, polite, patient, fun, and outgoing Andy.

I was not truthful and honest. While unable to control various emotions, addictions, actions, and responsibilities, my weak mind had continued to deteriorate. I was a broken spirit, consumed with self-loathing. But this experience showed me that if you open the passage to a clear mind, you can find ways out of any adverse situation.

AWAKENED BY THE THOUGHTS

"Free your mind, stretch beyond the heavens, and grow. Do not allow yourself to be content with the bare minimum in life."

Over the years, a condition had developed that I was scared to get diagnosed. It started as a rare occurrence, then, as years went by, it became frequent. A condition I had unknowingly developed with anxiety, fear, and worry. Dark, disturbing thoughts began to appear after my first son, Max, was born. Vivid thoughts of tragic events happening to my child, wife, loved ones, and extended family.

Whenever the thoughts appeared, a routine developed in my mind: I'd close my eyes, hover my tongue in the middle with my mouth shut, and shake my head from side to side a minimum of three times. If the thought worsened and were unbearable, I'd sometimes shake it more than five times. My mind told me this method was the only way to eliminate the dark thoughts. Wrath, worry, and fear are the work of the evil spirit to influence our lives into complete chaos.

My mind was frail and fragile. The evil spirit was welcomed. Wicked thoughts shaped my actions and attitude. Battling the demons with every traumatic experience fed the negativity, which grew stronger and stronger. I became bored with life and work; I was dangerous to myself. The more this life was darkened with negative energy, the more this soul faded into darkness. I felt enslaved to the dark.

Whispers of death are the only way out. Death will rid us of all our negative energy, negative thoughts, and sorrow. As our mind is weak, with no love and positive energy, we ultimately succumb to focusing on the negative.

When you have absolutely zero positivity, the love for yourself disappears. The mind and body lose their protection (positive energy), and the enemy swoops in with unlimited negativity. Hatred, resentment, fear, loneliness, selfishness, unwillingness, self-pity—every negative feeling we can imagine. As we are forced to focus only on that negative energy, our bodies and minds become consumed with evil, dark thoughts. We begin to lose all control while the evil spirit quickly infiltrates our minds and influences us with the solution of death.

Resilience in the face of adversity and further self-discovery have given me an entirely different outlook. I used to always think and say to myself, I hate my life. Why is this happening to me? Could it be because I have been sinning all my life? Why should good things happen when I do what I know is wrong?

These words will never have a place in this mind or be projected out of this mouth again. Self-pity, regret, and worry, while focusing on things I cannot control, have had an astronomical negative effect on me. It further restrained the progress of my relationships with those around me. I used to dwell on regrets, but those feelings are long gone and no longer occupy this space. I have learned to embrace my mistakes as valuable lessons.

FROM HOLLOWNESS TO LIFE

"I've come to you to unveil my dark secrets, to reveal all my sins."

I called my wife on my lunch break one day and told her we had to talk, to ensure I would follow through with the confession.

"Are you cheating on me?" she asked.

"No," I replied. "I would never do that."

"Are you gay?"

"No, honey," I giggled in response.

Apparently, those two things were what she feared most. Those must have been her deal-breakers.

This went on for minutes, as she insisted that I tell her immediately. I wanted to face the truth in person rather than hide behind the phone, but as ardent as she was, I finally gave in.

"Let me speak before you respond," I told her. "I want to confess all my darkest secrets. I'm sorry. I have been lying to you. I have stolen from you during hard times; I cheated in a past relationship; I supported two abortions; I have been irresponsible and mishandled our finances; I'm addicted to fantasy football and have spent thousands of dollars on it; I was addicted to porn; though you knew I took pills, you didn't know the extent of it—I was addicted to painkillers; my weed smoking has become uncontrollable."

After a brief pause, I continued, "Whatever you decide moving forward, I will accept and support. But know that you and the boys are my life."

I experienced an immediate release of burdens, afflictions, and negative energy from my body. I felt liberated from all forms of negativity, including hatred, pride, envy, shame, greed, lust, stress, and resentment. I was free from all falsehoods and deceit.

Within months, I had no desire or urge to watch

meaningless shows or movies or get on social media. I confidently made more responsible choices. We will be all right, I keep telling myself. All the while, my wife and I were happy and grateful. We spent more time with each other and the kids.

My wife, kids, and mother were happy and positive. The energy was dominant. I realized the negative energy had affected them greatly while I was going through the lowest point of my life. Upon facing the afflictions, in turn, it had healed and refined my weary soul. Unfortunately, it took a damaging experience for me to realize my life needed a drastic change.

MY TRUTH, MY SHAME

"Hiding my shame, addictions, and
faults from the world impedes my
progress for personal growth."

My confession to my wife was the hardest thing I had done in my life. I also admitted to her that my motivation for life had faded, and I had been an immoral person all my life, internally. I had essentially lived a lie.

Why the need to confess? That question circulated through my mind constantly. The fear of losing my wife was heavy. I realized that confessing to my wife was necessary, as it would open the path to releasing the burdens. Confessing my truth freed me from my sins. I acknowledged the importance of confessing to a priest. However, I felt that confessing to a priest would yield a different fear and not bear the same risk. It would allow me to hide from my shame.

I asked God to give me the strength to forgive myself for all my sins, so that I may be capable of loving and receiving love. I had to surrender my shame, guilt, and humility. The journey had begun.

Blessed with the revelation of confession and its power, I eliminated pride from my soul and life. This was the inner source of my well-being. It helped relieve stress and gave me ultimate access to my true self. Feeling liberated, I had conquered my fear—born again, with a clean slate, a chance to relive my life. Humbleness and gratitude began trickling in.

I became passionate again. I was and am passionate about becoming a better person and continuing this path for society, humanity, and my children, family, friends, and wife. Flushed with forgiveness, my body gave me a better understanding and inner resources to pursue the meaning of life. The path of forgiveness for my sins was my redemption. I sought to be a better person: father, husband, and son. Being ashamed of my sins enabled their control over me. Getting rid of this shame permitted me to live a better life and to be the best version of myself.

I realized everyone has their journey while the path has been laid before them. We all have the same journey, but the paths differ as we interpret life differently—a feeling of tremendous euphoria, of great accomplishment. The newfound revelation has led me here. We go through stages in our lives. We must find our heaven, our balance, and our true happiness.

By embracing life with positivity and forgiveness, I felt more in control of my emotions and thoughts. My mind is now unequivocal when making sound judgments and more responsible choices and decisions. I want to better myself as a person. I am capable of making better choices to make my life less stressful. No one can force you to do that but yourself. I now walk the path to truth, love, and forgiveness. Strengthen your mind; only then will you find your path.

CHAPTER FOUR

FREED FROM THE BURDENS OF HATRED

FORGIVING MYSELF

*"I surrendered pride, shame, and hate;
now I know only forgiveness."*

I PICKED UP FOOD ONE day at my sister Lynn's house. I have looked up to Lynn all my life. Our relationship was more mother-son than brother-sister, as she had cared for me since childhood. A sense of vulnerability and pity surfaced when she handed me the food. Instantly, I felt disgusted for the loathing I had for my sister. The anger and intense displeasure had taken complete control of my body. I blamed and resented her for my current situation and business handling. My demeanor toward her in the months during the closure of the business was harsh and unpleasant.

The path to forgiveness had revealed itself—ask forgiveness for the harbored hatred. I caught my sister off guard the following day with my confession and asked for forgiveness. We talked and passionately shared our feelings. Lynn said she understood the behavior and the stress I was dealing with, and she had given me space. On the other hand, I didn't recognize her stress and selfishly focused on myself.

As I confessed, the atmosphere filled with positive energy, and I could feel her relief. The exchange revived and heightened our relationship. This confession was instrumental in alleviating the weight of resentment and blame.

Feeling gratified and alive after the exchange, I ran rampant with the urge to pursue forgiveness.

Reflecting on how I responded to my niece, Lily, and how she handled her marriage, I realized I had selfishly put my feelings before hers. Even though we reconciled our relationship after a year of silence, and time had slowly pieced our love and respect for one another back together, the need to ask her for forgiveness was evident. Our relationship reached new heights, and the bond was enhanced by later talks of forgiveness, family, and her son, Jayce.

As she shared her life struggles, I shared my recent life change with the acceptance of faith—how it changed my whole life. Faith allowed my heart to forgive, not just repeat the words but live them, to vulnerably surrender myself to forgive. The Lord has forgiven me. I forgive myself.

THE REDEMPTION CONVERSATION

> *"May your demons meet with force,*
> *hatred meet with mercy, and every*
> *moment meet with love and joy."*

The journey of forgiveness persisted, and I reached out to an ex-girlfriend who had inflicted pain and hurt on me. She was my first love, the first committed relationship of four years. I could not imagine having positive or happy feelings for her again, as I was holding a grudge.

"Why would you want to open up old wounds?" my wife asked calmly. I did not reply at that moment.

Faced with a slight negative energy, the negative thoughts appeared: Am I jeopardizing and interfering with one's current happy life for my well-being, self-discovery, and inner peace? Am I opening past wounds to ask for forgiveness from past relationships, friends, and exes? It has been years, almost twenty.

About a minute passed and it dawned on me and I responded to my wife, "I have faith that she will positively receive this message." This was my way of erasing the pain, hurt, hatred, and resentment from my mind and body.

With the pursuit of faith, worries about how negatively she would respond were inconsequential. Fate had kept us as online friends all these years, living our separate lives. I proceeded to reach out to her on Messenger, as this was our only form of contact.

"Hey, how are you? This is quite random, but this is all positive. I would like to say sorry and ask for your forgiveness for all the things that happened in the past. I'm truly sorry for the outcome between us. I was wrong about how I handled things. I'm in a different place now. Back then, I was wrong for hating you; my heart was filled with hurt, hate, betrayal, and negativity. I was in a dark place at times; I wished in my mind that you would leave me because I was weak. This is my truth, and I wanted to share it with you. I am getting rid of all this negative energy and hate from my mind, body, and soul. You taught me to be a better man, and for that, I thank you. Please tell your husband there is no disrespect from me contacting you, no negativity. There's no need to respond. I see you are happy now with a great family, and I'm truly happy for you. The kids are beautiful. I know you two will teach them well. I hope one day you will see it in your heart to forgive me for my past sins and my hatred, and if that day never comes, it's totally OK. If we ever cross paths again in this lifetime, I know it will be positive. Say hello to your dad, his family, mother, and stepfather. I wish you and your family well..."

Three days later, she responded, "Hey, random boy, I appreciate you. I think it would be super healing for both of us if we could chat. I completely understand if you don't feel it is necessary. I want to be respectful of you and your family."

"Anytime! It's all good and positive! Also, make sure it's totally fine with your husband!"

"Yes, of course! He trusts me, and honestly, I trust myself, knowing that the intent is positive and nothing malicious."

We exchanged numbers and agreed to talk in a few hours. A quick, exhilarating hour went by as we chatted on the phone.

Sharing our past experiences and feelings, I sensed her growth without resentment. We talked about our families, children, and current lives. After the joyous conversation, the steadiness to stay on this path of truth and forgiveness amplified.

"So happy to talk to you; remember to give yourself grace as you continue on this journey and start living," my ex texted moments after our conversation.

How do we begin to find love and positivity in others who have inflicted pain, aggression, insults, and negative energy on us? How do we begin to search for and control those feelings and emotions?

ASKING FOR FORGIVENESS

"How do we repent? How do
we forgive ourselves?"

Lightened by the burdens, I found the strength to contact an ex-best friend, who I had not spoken to for more than seven years, to confess and ask for forgiveness. Hate, resentment, and blaming him for his failed marriage prevented me from reaching out sooner. I had abandoned my friend. I dismissed his pain and sorrow and placed my opinions and selfish feelings before his.

I called him, as he still had the same number, but there was no answer. Shortly, he texted back that he was going over homework with his baby girl and would text back. I waited till the following day and reached out again. At that point, I understood his hesitation in answering the phone call. Finally, I viewed it with love and positivity instead of negativity. Maybe he was still uncomfortable talking to me? I proceeded to text the confession—all the pain, hatred, resentment, and blame I had for him. I had blamed him for our fallout. I'd condemned him for his poor choices and for losing his second family, us. I was wrong.

Negative energy was nonexistent in the text. I was truthful about my feelings—soft and positive with my words:

"I understand you may be uncomfortable with me calling out the blue; of course, I would rather say this on the phone. I am sorry for what transpired in the past. I'm sorry for what happened between you and your wife and with the family. I was filled with hate and negativity toward you. I blamed you for what happened, and I am truly sorry for that. I'm in a different place now, mentally and spiritually. For me to forgive myself for my past sins and hate, I must erase and get rid of all this hate, resentment, and negative energy toward you, and anyone for that matter. I heard you moved to the Gulf Coast. I am genuinely happy for you and wish you and your family the best. I have no hate or negativity toward you anymore, and I hope you will forgive me one day. If not, that's OK, and there's no need to respond. If you do, that's fine too. I wish you well, brother."

A few hours later, he replied, "Just getting off work. Why did you have hatred and negativity toward me? What did I do?"

"It doesn't matter anymore, bro," I replied.

I continued, "I was wrong. I blamed you for the breakup of your marriage, and this is my confession, my truth, my evil, dark thoughts. My reason for wanting to talk back then was selfish and hateful. That was also wrong. We can now move forward with our lives without hate and resentment. I want to be the best person and version of Andy, the best husband, father, son, and brother. To achieve that, I need to forgive myself and ask for forgiveness from those I mistreated—all positive energy, bro. I love you. And maybe we will be brothers in the next life if not this one."

I felt his sincerity, as he wrote back, "No need to apologize. I hold no grudges. I went through my phases, too. I was angry and confused at first, then sadness, then disappointment and resentment, but I had to let go, and now there are no hard feelings anymore toward anyone. We go through what we go through to come out the other side if we ever do, and who we come out with. I went into my dark time alone, and came out alone. I was sad about that because I really needed my friends and my second family at the time, but all I had was myself. In those few years, I lost my friends, my wife, my kid, my new career, my business, my dad, my home, and almost my mind. All I needed at the time was a friend. But I had to realize all I had and needed was myself. So I can't be mad at anyone or rely on anyone to help me with my drama or downfall, so if you are looking for peace in all this, then I think you are OK on this end, and from what I can see, you are a good father and husband. Max and Micah are great young boys. Very respectful. I love them! So good luck, bro. Keep up with your journey."

I ended our conversation with the following, "Thank you. I'm truly happy to hear that from you. That's growth. We cannot change or focus on the past, but we can control and manifest what we do in the future. When we can no longer change or control a situation, we are tested by changing ourselves. Focus on the things we can control—our feelings, emotions, and minds—rather than try to control what we cannot. We have the power over our minds, not outside events. Realize this, and we can find strength. I wish I had known and understood this before. I wish you well, brother."

After exchanging messages with my ex-best friend, I felt lighter, even more than before. This gave me the strength to continue this path of truth and forgiveness. The path is strong. The will is strong.

The final confession was to my ex-girlfriend in Las Vegas. Ignorant and simple-minded, I cowardly cheated on her to purposefully end the relationship, which I had tried to exit before. The deranged thinking was that it would shift the hurt, pain, anger, and hatred toward me to help her find the strength to leave. I did not want her to think she was not good enough and lose self-confidence.

Perhaps the actions resulted from the pain I was feeling at that moment. Moreover, my arrogance clouded my judgment, and I thought the act was justified and honorable. But later I regarded myself as a horrible person, not only because I cheated but I had been dishonest with everyone. I created an image of a virtuous, truthful, decent person who despised infidelity, when in reality I was unfaithful.

I wrote a similar message to my ex in Vegas to confess and ask for forgiveness, as I continued on this path.

UNSHACKLED FROM SIN

*"Our sins and afflictions prevent us
from obtaining forgiveness."*

I came across a story about a man who had the strength to forgive his estranged father, who'd inflicted physical and mental abuse on him when he was a child. The son had forgiven his father and grew up to become a preacher. He

50

did not allow his traumatic childhood to negatively affect him. It was not until the father was on his deathbed that he finally comprehended the true extent of his son's forgiveness.

"Can you forgive me?" the father asked his son. With guilt, remorse, and regret, the father apologized with praise and dignity.

By freeing themselves from the weight of their past, they found redemption and purpose—and passed hope to the youth for a brighter future. Inspiring, true stories like these expanded my faith and served as a potent reminder that forgiveness is a gift that should be valued and that it is never too late to seek redemption and start anew.

I acknowledged my inability to forgive and my self-ishness. Being trapped by sins had burdened my ability to forgive, eventually hindering my potential to progress and improve. I envisioned putting myself in the shoes of those I felt animosity toward or who had treated me unfairly. If they were on their deathbed, all the hurtful things they'd said or done would become insignificant. I could whole-heartedly forgive them. I could cultivate and apply that same sense of forgiveness right now instead of waiting for that moment in the future.

I had only used the word "forgiveness" but never truly felt its meaning. I felt absolute truth and righteousness. The power of forgiveness opened my eyes to a whole new world.

Pride would have prevented me from confessing to my wife or myself, but forgiveness conquered and replaced my ego. Forgiving had become second nature. I was freed from the burden of my sins—negative energy, pain, suffering, anger, and hate. Free from all the burdens, I am now able to love, forgive, self-improve, learn, and try to be perfect.

The inability to forgive others hurts us more than them. Eventually, this creates further conflicts that separate us from achieving inner peace. No feelings of anger, hatred, or disrespect will matter in ten or twenty years. The burdens you carry can negatively affect your entire life. We wait for tragedy, failure, depression, or hurt to give us a reason to change. Some cannot overcome that hurt. Love yourself. Forgive yourself. Only when we forgive ourselves will we have the strength to ask for forgiveness from others, even though they may have no idea how we feel. Approach it positively, and they will receive it as such. These positive thoughts and energy become a choice and can project out of our bodies. Our positive energy can touch others.

Forgiveness is a worthwhile emotion that requires effort. It is natural to feel a strong urge and demand for revenge when someone has wronged us, but acting on this impulse is only destructive to ourselves. Instead, forgiveness demands a deep understanding of yourself and others, a willingness to empathize and the wisdom to let go. It is a powerful act of compassion that can bring peace and freedom to both parties. Seek and free yourself of the burdens of hate and bondage.

CHAPTER FIVE

CHAPTER FIVE

EXPERIENCING
THE PRESENCE

FAITH FOUND ME

"I fell in love with God."

"ANDY, I NEVER TOLD you this, but years ago I prayed that you would one day discover your faith," a long-time client and friend revealed to me.

"Thank you," I replied softly. "I am grateful for your prayers. They came true, Mrs. Haley."

While I have been Haley's nail technician for more than ten years, we had never discussed our faith or mentioned any religious topics. Seemingly, my sinful lifestyle and choices had contributed to my apathy toward religion...until the blissful day that I shared my testimony of faith—accepting God and Jesus Christ into my life—and she was thrilled to confess her secret prayers for me. With her Christian background, her genuine, mindful nature guided her to pray rather than forcing faith on me, and our relationship has transcended to another spiritual level.

I began praying for others after Haley unveiled her kind-hearted prayers for me. I followed her example, which also strengthened my faith in myself. Now, praying for others has shifted to praying that God be welcomed into the lives of others, as then everything will fall into place.

Christ, a perfect soul, is known to have lived a sinless life while on Earth and performed his work flawlessly in human form, yet he still prayed to God. This shows that even the Son of God acknowledged the importance of having a relationship with our Father through prayer. In the same way, when faced with difficult situations that require courage and strength, solace is found in praying. Like our Lord, who prayed fervently in the Garden of Gethsemane before his crucifixion, I found the courage to pray—and mustered the valor to face my fears through prayer.

For the first time, my prayers to God came from a truthful place within my heart. I discovered that these prayers would be heard and answered with faith, while the inner demons perished. Prayer is a powerful tool that can help us navigate life's challenges and draw us closer to God.

I had no interest in religion and the Bible in the past. I was looking for the flaws in Christ, as I had looked for the flaws in the Bible. My refusal to acknowledge religion altogether created a feeling of uncomfortableness and uneducated. I was consumed with meaningless self-interest and indulged in material possessions and greed. I was influenced by society while simultaneously affecting it. My sudden pursuit of faith and understanding of the Bible resulted from the power of prayers.

As an average, uneducated nail technician from Vietnam, my journey toward purpose was steered by faith. When faced with life's struggles, I was on the verge of self-destruction, and no one could help me but me. I gave up on trying to live—almost entirely. Seeking help from the spiritual world was the only way out. I would never have considered confessing to my wife if rock bottom had not been touched. A sunken ship with the treasures of a caring wife, two beautiful kids, a home, and a career.

I was detached from spirituality and had nowhere to turn, so I reached out to God. My life needed to change, and I was delicately guided to faith. It took me twenty years to attend Word of Life Church and my whole life to accept Christ and welcome God. It was, in the end, a simple decision—nothing remarkable, just an added soul to God's kingdom. I felt the sudden joy of His love.

Attending church is an opportunity for spiritual growth and reflection, but the act of attending itself does not constitute, warrant, or guarantee personal change. Change must come from within. The church is there to encourage, give hope, and remind us that we have a choice.

The longing for a better life for my wife, children, boys, and family fueled the desire to improve. Discovering faith transformed me, despite being an ordinary man living an ordinary life, leading to self-discovery and self-improvement. It is incredible how something so simple as faith can make such a profound difference. Faith gave me the ambition to improve and live again. The intent behind my ambition was healthy. Before reading the Bible or learning detailed facts about Him, I felt a deep trust in Him within my heart. I fell in love with our Lord.

We often deviate from our paths, and even when we finally realize the path we are on, we constantly face challenges to make informed decisions, good or evil. Negative life situations and struggles can lead one astray. This is evident in every aspect of life, including religion, spirituality, health, career, finance, family, and relationships.

IN PURSUIT OF SOMETHING GREATER THAN MYSELF

"There is only one name."

At forty-one, having acquired faith, I attended my first Bible study at Word of Life. Expectations were met with excitement as I stepped foot into a small house where the study was held. While the house began to fill up with what seemed like college students, I felt a little out of place. My past prideful self would have left early. But this time, I stayed and listened for three hours, feeling exuberant with the sentiment of understanding the Bible's words and eager to learn more.

It was quite clean with a scent of fresh air compared to the last time I stepped foot in a college house. Everyone seemed friendly and greeted me with life and gratitude, while bringing food and snacks for the study. I was quite impressed by the young adults who had crowded the small living room, willing to take time out of their busy lives to better themselves. We started to circulate the room to introduce ourselves. One by one, I could sense confidence and gratefulness in their calm, mild tone while we prayed and discussed the Scriptures. But as we went into the night, their confidence was overshadowed by their unfortunate stories and struggles. I learned much from them as they discussed and shared their hardships and prayers.

This experience strengthened my path toward faith. I had never felt the need to read the Bible, and did not own one. Although I'd heard the Scriptures, quotes, and lessons throughout my life, I never understood their meaning or how to put them into action. I had never experienced the words; therefore, they were meaningless to these ears.

When I was growing up, no one was able to help me understand the Scriptures. It was not until my spirit was ready to accept that I finally comprehended their meaning. When we are open and willing to receive, we come to understand the true significance behind seemingly simple sayings, such as "forgive one another" and "forgive ourselves." The most impactful quotes and phrases were ordinary words with powerful meanings. Simple words and sayings can have a profound impact when we are ready for them.

Hearing the words was easy, but understanding and applying them seemed impossible, so I focused only on manageable tasks. I attempted to force myself to decipher complex, intellectual sentences and sayings to feel educated, but I could never apply them to my life. They impacted me only momentarily, and I returned to my old self. Ultimately, I grasped the enduring significance of the message carried by these words, regardless of their arrangement. Words were no longer just words—they came alive and became transparent and precise when applied to everyday life. The gift of righteousness had been received.

Don't just hear the words. Live them.

As I became familiarized with the words of the Bible, I began to relate more and more to the stories and Scriptures. I connected the thoughts and experiences to the teachings with each new verse. Through these experiences, I was blessed to understand the Bible's meanings, values, and lessons. And though I desired to share my sensations of the Bible's words with others, I realized that it was not within my control to make them understand.

The light was unveiled. With God's will, I knew that His words were true and flawlessly pure in intent. Understanding the Lord's truth, my truth, gave me stability. The confession was the submission, submitting to God's word so I would be welcomed and live in His kingdom. The mercy was the freeing of burdens. The gift was the ability to forgive, and faith was the gate to heaven. Jesus Christ had healed and refined my soul.

While my faith grew stronger, it gave me access to speak about it courageously and not hide from it. I used to be intimidated by those who knew more about religion and faith than I did. I was hesitant and distanced myself from them. Having minimal knowledge of any religion or faith, I averted the conversations and interactions. The fear of wrongly using words and their possible reactions made me even more reluctant.

But faith replaced fear, dismay, and inadequacy. I am now committed to constantly improving mentally and spiritually, and I am a student of religion and myself. I will continue to surround myself with positivity. Faith was found within, and I am grateful for the strength it gave me. I thank God for my acceptance of life's challenges and for my ability to capture joy amid adversity. I trust Him to guide me with thoughts, words, and understanding that are not my own.

I had always been in the vicinity of faith but never fully understood its power, as I was never committed to it. However, there were some minor signs that I overlooked, such as attending youth church functions, marrying a Chinese Baptist from Greenville, Mississippi, and having longtime clients like Dorothy (Momma Dot) and Pastor Jennifer. I also sent my children to a Christian-based private school, and my youngest child, Micah, was fascinated with rainbows at an early age. (The rainbow, of course, is a symbol of God's covenant.) Despite not realizing it at the time, these experiences significantly impacted my life and helped me discover my faith. Undeniably, faith has brought many meaningful friendships to my doorstep, including Haley, who confessed her secret prayers and ignited my pursuit of faith, which has now been fulfilled.

POSITIVE ENERGY

"Truth and positivity will result in positive outcomes."

One day, while getting the mail, I noticed that the front, right side of the lawn was flush with green grass. I was shocked and excited, as that part of the lawn had been mainly dirt. It had been bald and brutal for almost two years, as I tried everything, including water, fertilizer, and other treatments. Ecstatic, I took a picture and showed it to my family and friends.

"Those are weeds, Andy," said Ross, who used to own a small lawn-care business.

"It does not matter if it's weed or grass; it's green and growing," I replied enthusiastically. "Where were the weeds last year? Where were they two years ago?"

Scorching and in a drought for weeks, Mississippi had broken records for the hottest summer in decades. I concluded that this small miracle (green on that part of the lawn) resulted from the positive energy I'd had the last few weeks.

Now I look back at the negative energy I'd previously brought home. The house was always messy, the children constantly fought, and my wife complained frequently. My mother was constantly in pain, unmotivated, and lacking energy. The yard was unattractive and dead, and the house was unhappy. That energy and frequency affected every aspect of the home and everyone in it.

Unfavorable experiences occurred. You could call it bad luck. My mother, along with her newly discovered rare illnesses, got into a car accident. The house began to fall apart, and major appliances stopped working. My old vehicle finally broke down in the middle of the highway. We found out our youngest child is slightly deaf in both ears and we began to inquire about treatments and hearing aids. As these experiences and occurrences added to my stress, I began to find my path.

Within months, my whole life and outlook had changed. Positive energy was plentiful throughout the home, and it became a paradise. We had created heaven. I was genuinely happy, motivated, stress-free, worry-free, and full of life and positive energy. That energy followed me to work, the gym, to visit friends and family, home, and everywhere I went. Why am I not tired? Where is this energy coming from?

Promising experiences and occurrences began to happen. My mother became healthier and happier and yelled less often. Her garden flourished, when we could never grow anything in the past. The children argued less, the wife was happier, and the complaints were minimal. The business became successful. I even noticed that my employee, Wendy, had been more cheerful—energy emanated from her frequent smile, which was rare before. The positive energy reached my best friend Angela, whom I have known for almost twenty years. She started reconnecting with me comfortably. She began calling every morning as we drove our kids to school, sharing her little moments of joy, like she used to.

But even emptied of hatred and negative energy, I knew the evil spirit never rests. It is always there, knocking on the door, pounding the mind, and creating dark thoughts. I am strong enough to battle and block out these thoughts, I told myself each morning. Let's have a good day, positive energy, positive thoughts, and positive words. Control your emotions and views with love, empathy, and forgiveness. I never knew that daily affirmations could yield such vigor.

Positivity results in positive outcomes. Even with a negative response, we can manipulate negativity into positivity.

Being positive and thinking positively does not necessarily mean ignoring your problems and negative situations. Approach those situations positively, eliminating stress to make clearer and better choices. We have heard all our lives that when it rains, it pours. It does not rain any more. It is all sunshine and rainbows. Every day is a good day when you are living in the presence of God.

TO LIVE MEANINGFULLY WITH GOD

"I am in control of my destiny;
faith will decide my fate."

God sacrificed his perfect son. Every day, I remember that Christ died for our sins. Therefore, obey the commandments and follow the way of Christ. Sin is powerful, an evil spirit, but that negative energy lifted when I confessed to my wife. With God within me, I can forgive myself and others. I have accepted God, Christ, and truth.

Now I understand the meaning of having a relationship with Christ. A path is walked—and that path is the relationship. I keep hearing those positive words: Continue down the path. But negative words constantly try to take me off the path.

I was born again—the feeling of a cleansed, perfect spirit striving toward righteousness. However, by nature, our mind and body will always be bound to sin. Our sinful nature enslaves us to it. Through our Lord, we can find balance. Without a relationship with God, we cannot reach eternal life. Self-destruction leads to death, which leads to separation from God. Faith is my pill, my path to progress.

I now see that sin handicaps our ability to control ourselves and our lives. The weight of our sin affects us; heavy hearts become incapable of true happiness, forgiveness, and peace. Consequently, we transform into darkness. Saturated with pain, anger, and resentment, we can become unpleasant to be around.

I fully understand the significance of confessing one's sins, living through them, and experiencing the power of these words. Confessing my sins and secrets was the first step in acknowledging my flaws and mistakes: I have sinned. Had I not admitted to my wife the suppressed animosity, unsettling thoughts, secrets, and wrongdoings, I would have inevitably spiraled into self-destruction. That is how close it came. Accepting Christ was my mercy—a new start. This book is God's mercy.

According to my laws, morals, and values, I tried to live this life correctly and failed miserably. It was not until I lived with God's law that I found peace and purpose—freed from my sins. I now live to succeed for others, not myself. I strive for a life without sin. I hope that others will notice and follow.

I have received the power of the Holy Spirit. This power enables me to forgive others, empathize with those around me, show compassion, overcome my addictions, refrain from passing judgment, and pursue life and not sin. I feel the ultimate confidence to rebound and attack life, though realizing this feeling might not last long enough to condition my mind. As long as there is faith, it will continue to guide my mind to eternal life.

Steadfast on the path to heaven, I strive to live a truthful life of righteousness, sinlessness, forgiveness, and empathy—to strive for perfection. I aim to live in the present reality, spiritually connected to the world. I use the teachings as strength, for I may stray from the path at any moment. Going to church does not guarantee me a place in heaven. I must bring the experience of church home with me and carry it everywhere I go, in order to achieve an everlasting relationship with God and for my thoughts to be influenced by the teachings and guidance of our Lord, not the evil spirit.

When we come to this revelation, we can control and manifest positive, successful relationships with family, friends, and strangers and adapt to the world's darkness. We are capable of achieving peace and positivity in the world. Repent. Forgive yourself for past sins as God forgives us. Follow the path of righteousness as the word of Christ guides us to heaven—to eternal life.

I have repented of my ways, thoughts, and life, turning to God and faith.

I have recognized all my sins,

I have sorrow for my sins,

I have forsaken my sins,

I have confessed my sins,

I have made restitution,

I have forgiven others,

I will keep the commandments of God.

CHAPTER SIX

LIFE'S BLESSINGS AND CURSES

'WE DO NOT USE THE 'D' WORD.'

*"The words we use have power
and impact our actions."*

WHILE LANGUAGE CONSTANTLY EVOLVES, I am continually challenged to change my vocabulary to be more positive. Occasionally, I have used the word "devil" to refer to evil-influenced actions, as it has been a common term throughout history. However, a new friend and client, Rhonda, shared her perspective on the word.

"We do not use the 'D' word in our household, Andy."

As our relationship developed over the past year, her words resonated. Then one day, when I was mowing the lawn, the meaning of her words finally clicked. I realized that using that word gives power and praise to the negative energy it represents and that I did not want to contribute to that; I do not worship that spirit. So the "D" word has been removed from my vocabulary and replaced with other words.

I have also struggled to take a more cognitive approach to language use. My frequent use of "negative" has established a connotation similar to "evil." The more I have used the word "negative" to describe specific thoughts and actions, the deeper, more unconstructive meaning it possesses. It creates further judgment. Finding the balance of words is crucial.

In the past, nobody could force understanding on me or help me comprehend the Scriptures. When I was ready to accept it, it was finally understood. The words were not meant for the old me, who had been unreceptive to the messages, but for the new me.

Our language has been simplified and dumbed down, with words becoming meaningless and often accompanied by aggression and hate. As a product of my environment and our modern societal influence on education and religion, it deterred me from the Bible, faith, and the path. I felt less educated trying to understand the words, as I became simpler and separated from the true sense of life.

Speech often influences our behavior; our actions are led by our words. The words we choose reflect our beliefs and attitudes, and they can profoundly impact how we behave. The power of language lies in its ability to inspire, motivate, and persuade us to act. We should be mindful of the words we use and the messages we convey, as they, too, can affect the behavior of those around us. By choosing our words carefully, we can create a more positive and impactful environment that encourages growth, collaboration, and mutual understanding.

REFLECTIONS OF MY SOUL

*"I am an existence that does not conform
to anything or any standard of myself."*

The essence of who I am is intricately woven into the fabric of my life, influenced by my circumstances, experiences, relationships, and interactions with the world around me. Despite these influences, I remain unbound by any single definition or expectation complementary to shaping my identity and purpose. As I must be consistent, I can be as educated or foolish as I want and become whatever I choose.

Like many others, I have watched the movie *Forrest Gump* more times than I can count. The title character's unconventional behaviors and mindset were challenging for me to understand. I could never relate to them before. As I was engrossed in the film the last time I watched it, I could not help but feel a strong sense of connection to the character. To some degree, I felt like I had been living a similar life to him. Despite lacking the same level of recognition and without the character's accolades, I identified with his traits of authenticity, humility, purity, and the absence of anxiety and pressure. The character reflected my life. Even when struck with troubled times and the tragedy of his mother's death, he overcame the experience with love and positivity.

Well into my journey, only one person thoroughly asked how I came to the current path and the process of changing who I am.

"I'm happy for you," "Congratulations," and "I'm proud of you" were the common responses to my life change. But this particular client was eagerly seeking direction to change her life. I could tell she was earnestly pursuing her path. Not only was she happy to see my change, but she desired the same. She had been absent from the salon for a while, and when she returned we began to share updates about our lives. She became engaged in the conversation. Her first question was how I got to where I am currently at. She followed with many questions about my motivation and why I changed. "Faith" was my answer. I told her I had changed for God. Changing solely for me had not been successful because I had worshipped myself; I needed to change for my children and her children. I further explained the details of my transformation of accepting Jesus into my life.

Despite hearing stories and experiences of people being born again and changing their lives, I had never felt the need to reflect on my life and consider making changes. While I was aware of personal transformation, it had never resonated with me, and I had never felt motivated to explore it further.

Life had always been straightforward, and I had been complacent to simply live as is, without trying to alter anything. However, I now acknowledge that everyone's journey is different, and personal transformation can be a powerful and life-changing experience.

Throughout the years, I have encountered many great minds, pure and genuine. I have always wondered how I could imitate one's genuine character traits if I was untrustworthy. I would be a fraud if I were to depict similar characteristics. I wanted to be pure, authentic, and honest. But how could I become that person with all my flaws?

It dawned on me why my friends had jokingly called me "thunder stealer." Craving to be the center of attention, pride dictated my personality. I now realize that personality traits can be altered. As I lived inconsistently, I was inconsistent with good choices and consistent with sinning.

Further understanding one's traits may prevent us from struggling. Good character traits constitute consistency, while bad ones are inconsistent. Question everything for consistency and truth. Will it withstand the scrutiny?

Who am I? Who was I? Am I pretending to be someone I am not? These questions once had life and power. Who I was for so long does not constitute who I am now. I am a progressing mind and spirit. I am a developing person who is becoming more than I had been accustomed to—not like anyone or anything else.

Who I am now is the person I pretended and portrayed to be all my life, the person I have always desired to be. My mind has been freed, unbound. I am free to choose a better life; this is who I am.

Once a negative thought or idea has been fixed upon a person or thing, we become incapable of generating positive thoughts. We must look at and assess the situation with positive feelings toward that person or subject rather than with negative emotions. Compare the two emotions. Which one holds more value? You will always take the opposing side when you dislike someone, even when they are doing good. When you favor someone, you will always see the good in them. Make excuses for them, defend them, and see the positive in any situation.

I thought I was perfect by replying "perfect" when someone asked, "How are you?" I had lied to myself every day that I did not need to improve and was simply fine and content with how I was. Perfectly flawed—we have allowed sins to infiltrate our everyday lives. Sinning becomes normalized through society, upheld as a value, as a trend, and we begin to praise sin. Pursue greatness. Pursue a sinless life.

I never acknowledged my struggle with anxiety, as my sister Nina has pointed out to me over the years. The failure to recognize the issue was concealed by pride and stubbornness. Denial was second nature, as if nothing was wrong with me, as if nothing needed improvement. I realized I hindered myself from acknowledging the indisputable fact that I was unaware of my anxiety. Constrained by the demons of pride, I could not uncover the hard truth, the refusal to receive constructive criticism and teaching. The dark spirit had infiltrated my mind and influenced me to believe that this was who I was, and I was powerless to change. I finally understood the meaning of loving yourself. I had fallen in love with pride, not my soul. I have surrendered to and love Christ, not my personal desires and flesh.

Pride strangleholds change. Not changing how we think, talk, and feel ultimately limits our attempts at new things. Improving ourselves becomes an afterthought. The most basic value of life is the most difficult to achieve. To become a good person with righteous moral values and truth—live in peace, tranquility, and love.

THE INFLUENCE OF GREED

"Overcome the desires of wealth and riches;
only then will you truly begin to enjoy life."

The more I focus on the financial stress and life's failures, the more I covet the winning lottery ticket. I enabled the idea to hope for wealth. A false sense of hope, as the dark spirit sways it. And if I did win, attaining immediate riches may hinder my personal growth. It would probably influence me to walk away from God and, eventually, this book. The old Andy would, once more, take over this mind. Again, this hinders my full potential.

The obsession with purchasing lottery tickets in hopes of chasing immediate wealth is no longer present; I want to earn it. Financial success and well-being are within my grasp. My mind is the winning ticket to success. Staying on the path, the desire to win the lottery waned. By practicing greater financial discipline and responsibility while productively utilizing time, I understand what living in the present moment truly means.

I stubbornly looked up to those with wealth and high financial status and looked down on those with lesser means. The impression was that greatness was showcased through wealth. The wealthy were thought to be wise and educated. I envied those with wealth, thinking the status was reached with some form of education and some degree of intelligence, which is only sometimes the case. Wise minds come in all types.

I clearly remember that, at times, I would hear words of knowledge and wisdom but could focus only on who they were coming from, overlooking the content and meaning. My negative self valued words only from success and belittled the words of the less successful. I judged their worthiness according to their financial success and achievements. Again, my judgment of those I gave respect to and sought it from was flawed.

At the peak, I was making well over one hundred fifty thousand a year. The money came with a sense of power, confidence, and accomplishment, which added to my arrogance. Fueled by greed, I ventured into the stock market during the COVID lockdown of 2020. I made more money than I had ever dreamed of, though it was briefly maintained due to poor self-control. The excessive ego had led to heightened vanity and an inflated sense of self-importance.

Greed and self-glory began to block the willingness to be receptive to critiques and further knowledge. I failed to isolate myself from the influences of fear, greed, and pride. Reaching financial stability, the pride was at its strongest. Ironically, the arrogance had cheated me from progressing. The flaw in my generosity had hampered my ability to make responsible financial decisions.

I was living beyond my means, spending recklessly, and hurting financially to personify as a generous, well-off person. Due to irresponsible choices, a sea of debt was acquired. Showing high status and financial stability is how I thought I would gain respect—pretending to be rich and upper class. Seeking respect through untruthfully displaying wealth was my flaw—respect is earned through other means.

Money brought only false hope and promises disguised as happiness. There are things in this life that money cannot fix and resolve; all it did was help suppress and forget the troubles. Thinking luxury things could make me happy—feeding pride with material things—I had found false glee. Once vanity had departed, those desires were no longer desirable.

Wealth comes in all forms and can be obtained without greed. Surviving the hunger of greed for success can be achieved. Although some may succeed with the powers of greed, the evil spirit preys on their weaknesses, and the weakness spreads, ultimately conforms, and leads to destruction.

The strength of my faith will not allow wealth and riches to control me. When wealth stumbles across my path, the content of my character will remain when the money disappears. The temptations of wealth and what it holds corrupt the purity of our souls.

CHAPTER SEVEN
THE 'AFTER'

ONLY HE CAN JUDGE

"We will cease to feel judged when we can genuinely liberate ourselves from judging others."

"**D**O YOU THINK I am wrong for yelling?" my wife asked me one day after disciplining Max for irritating Micah. The question was prompted after I quietly waited to talk to Max in a different tone.

I paused and took my time to carefully find the words to respond, as this question could yield complications. "I'm sorry," I said, "but I will not and cannot answer that question. Only you can answer it. If you think it's OK to yell, then it's OK. If you don't think it's OK to yell and choose not to, then don't—and that's OK, too. But I won't tell you if you're right or wrong for yelling." And I left it at that.

It was silent for a few moments, and without further affecting our emotions, we shifted to another subject.

I no longer view or engage in behaviors that I favored in the past. I used to smoke and yell, among other things, but realized that these behaviors were not good for me and did not align with my new understanding of values. Once they were considered sinful, I chose not to engage in them. But I do not judge others for their different perspectives and choices.

I do not view others negatively based on their choices, understanding that everyone has their circumstances and perspectives to consider. These newly acquired views and perspectives are not considered the "right" or "wrong" way. They are simply a different way of thinking and a different route of action. I do not desire to be better than anyone; I strive to be better than myself.

I have noticed that when sharing my opinions and outlook, others feel judged by me. It becomes a sin only if we doubt its morality and believe what we do is wrong but still engage in it.

If we do not consider an act sinful, it is not a sin in our understanding. Even with more severe acts like stealing, violence, and murder, we can tell the person it is wrong and a sin. But to them, in their mind, what they are doing is acceptable. They will understand the words only once they are at peace with their convictions.

We cannot tell others what they are doing is wrong and sinful. It implies judging them negatively. Our differences in personal philosophies and approaches to life situations do not warrant judgment of one another. We then submit to our nature to compare, which leaves us feeling unworthy and shameful. Comparison deprives us of joy and chips away at confidence and inherent self-worth. Through reflection, we aim to improve ourselves and become the best versions of ourselves.

The phrase "I judge with love" has also been removed from my vocabulary. I now view others with love and positivity.

Judgment insinuates that they have been living wrong and that I am above them; therefore, I judge them with love. God and I are the only ones who can judge me. Take the time to reflect on your beliefs and consider the consequences of your actions.

Judging others does not lead to personal growth or improvement. As such, it is not my place to pass judgment on others. I will never tell anyone what they are doing is wrong or insinuate judgment. Instead, I focus on self-improvement and encourage others to do the same. Ultimately, it is within everyone to judge what is right and wrong for themselves.

Whatever we do may bring about a sense of judgment from others. We judge ourselves, not them. We can give in, admit, and honestly reflect on our actions. Ask ourselves: Why do we feel judged? Is it others who are judging us, or are our guilt-driven thoughts performing the judgment? How do I know that they are judging me? Is it because we think we are doing something wrong? There may be a sense of doubt; therefore, our feeling of being judged stems from it.

Understand that no one can judge us, nor should they. People have unique perspectives, experiences, and beliefs that inform their choices and actions. Use your values and beliefs to identify what you consider negative and strive to make positive choices that align with your principles.

We can build a more tolerant and accepting world where everyone feels safe and respected—the power to stop feeling judged lies in our own hands. The feeling of judgment is the manifestation of our spiritual connection with God. His spirit in us is why we have those feelings.

Is it possible to not feel judged? Yes, because these feelings and thoughts are ours. They come from within us, not others. When we feel judged, it is us—God's judgment. He is the ultimate arbiter of our actions and decisions.

On some level, it has been a challenge to be mindful of those who have not been receptive to changes. I must consider how to share my experiences and opinions and be conscious of the choices of others, to convey the message as helpful and informative without appearing self-centered, to figure out how to share the journey toward a healthier lifestyle in a constructive way that can benefit others. I am now faced with the challenge of mindfully living in consideration of others.

MINDFUL LIVING

"There is no end to the passion for the courage to change and progress."

Whenever I came across various videos, teachings, and preaching, I should have considered the messages they conveyed. Instead, I carried on with my life. I often felt judged and hypocritical of those trying to teach me, considering that they, too, are sinners.

These feelings of self-judgment have noticeably disappeared, and forgiveness has long replaced them. Since the change, I have yet to feel judged by others. Judgment from others has lost its presence. It now rests with the Lord, along with my confession, shame, pride, and sins.

What constitutes good or bad judgment? Minor, unfavorable life decisions that may have been overlooked are no longer approved. However, I am still searching for the balance to live well and without feeling alienated. Pursued on this journey with a sudden burst of positive energy and full of life, I reacted and responded to releasing the energy by sharing this path and journey with others.

Being positive all the time can be seen as an annoyance. While receiving positive feedback from others has only strengthened my faith in staying on this path, others may perceive it somewhat negatively. Some interpret the newfound revelation as boasting that I am better than them, which makes them feel like a lesser person, inadequate, and in a negative light. No one has time to listen to how great of a person you have become, they may think.

I had mistakenly expressed the lifestyle changes by sharing improvements in physical and mental well-being;

the delivery came across as egotistical. Sincere words can be misheard as lecturing. Uncomfortable feelings about lecturing others have held back my desire to share words of help and encouragement. Although I wanted to share my experiences with others in hopes that they might be inspired to make similar changes in their lives, the sensitive nature of decisions that affect one's character has, at times, discouraged me from voicing my views. On the other hand, the silence may seem as though I am judging.

There is a balance between communicating my personal experiences and not sharing too much. Instead of vocalizing how I have quit my bad habits—consuming sugary and energy drinks, losing my temper, cursing, gambling, taking pills, smoking, etc.—I can live the lifestyle without mentioning and drawing attention to it.

"I'm on a new path. ..." That statement has ceased to exist. The more I state the phrase, the more self-praise is felt, even though that was not the intent. A whisper of pride gently touches the soul. I began questioning the words. I knew my heart was loving. I want to share my life and find diverse ways and approaches so we can embody positive energy together. I realized my paths could be shared with methods other than verbal. Sharing new views and perspectives through silence and actions has had more of a positive impact.

Amid the self-reflection induced by the immediate change in character, some may have viewed this as just a phase. And that's all right, as this phase has no end. Improving oneself sees no limit. I feel their self-reflection, comparing their lives while receiving my changes. Living a stress-less lifestyle may seem stressful to others. Conversely, I wrestle with attuning to the new mindset while still being considerate of their feelings and lifestyle.

What I perceive to be a well-lived life may differ from their perception. Sharing the different views and inputs gives the impression of being judgmental. I had expressed and exposed myself as the kind of person I have been—a faulty one living a life of lies. By comparison with similar behaviors, it would have meant that they, too, were not a good person. While their words of comfort and assurance that I was not a bad person were comforting and reassuring, their inner conflicts may be challenged while witnessing the changes. The new outlook has further separated my views and opinions from those of others.

How do you abruptly transition from a sinful lifestyle to seeking a sinless new life without being perceived as superior? How do we share a new life outlook without judgment? I have yet to uncover a convincing answer. Nonetheless, silence is the key and can be used as a form of speech.

Abruptly changing your life and outlook can have consequences. In contrast, while I became receptive to sudden life changes, the views, behavior, and faults in my generous nature extended to sharing my newfound life. Likewise, thoughts of winning the lottery would ensure the same act. However, not allowing ample time for others and me to adapt to the changes resulted in me mishandling how the experiences were shared.

Again, with repeated characteristic patterns, I have come across as too forceful with boundless positivity and optimistic words. I thought the positive attitude was a good thing. Looking back, I realize that the unbridled enthusiasm may have been overwhelming for others and could have been perceived as pushy or aggressive.

Acclimated to my limited and average intellect, sharing insight and joyful experiences may have been deemed self-glory and conceded to some, even with delicate words and tones. Others witness the changes, feeling inadequate, incompatible with the comparisons, and unable to change; hence, they judge themselves negatively. How do they reconcile and respond to your sudden changes?

They may wonder, "Should I be living my life better?" Am I a bad person? Our shared views and life choices embody these thoughts and questions, as does the feeling of conviction in one's judgment.

I confided in a dear friend about a significant change in my life. Our two-hour conversation led my friend, Pete, to open up about his personal experience and relationship with one of his closest friends, who I have never met.

The two friends have been inseparable for years despite leading different lifestyles. One is a minister with strong faith, while the other is a laid-back club owner who enjoys drinking alcohol, chasing women, and using profanity. The minister is a family man with different values, but he never judges his friend for his choices, nor does Pete compare and judge him for his. Although some people perceive them as the odd couple, their friendship remains strong. The two had been accustomed to each other's lives from the beginning—the adaptation was seamless. They have always accepted each other for who they are.

The conversation Pete and I had solidified the understanding that time holds great powers and can be used for our benefit. Changes will become familiar. Future relationships will be acquainted with new Andy in a way that is not comparable to the past.

I thought I needed to affirm to friends and family that the new path was necessary to notify them of the changes happening. While some have reacted positively, others have had mixed reactions. Indeed, I realize that it is no longer necessary to reassure anyone about my chosen path, whether they are old friends or new acquaintances. I stay patient and allow everyone, including myself, to acclimate to the change. Twenty years from now, friends and family will know and remember the new me.

How can I mindfully help and share this journey with the world when I have not found ways to share it with my family? I have asked myself this question repeatedly. As I have said, it can be challenging to voice our opinions and experiences to friends and loved ones without them feeling like we are trying to teach, preach, and lecture.

I can only share advice but cannot tell you what to say or do. Nor does it constitute a right or wrong way. The words come only when we completely control our feelings and emotions; the path will be clear. Our decisions will steer away from mixed and confused feelings. Following others' advice without truly believing in it and understanding ourselves further increases the chance of repeating old behaviors we try to eliminate.

All we can do is pray and lead by example. We can find strength and courage through faith to face life—to face others with different views and beliefs—mindfully. As my brother-in-law Jonathan tells me, "Silence is a language." Furthermore, time and silence will help share the path.

AN UNNATURAL EXPERIENCE

*"I can create heaven on Earth and
heaven in my mind, or hell."*

On August 27, 2023, I was sitting at the dining-room table. The computer was in front of me, water on the left and notes on the right. My hands were ready to draft for my fantasy leagues. Filled with positivity and excitement, I noticed my wife's low, dispassionate energy. I told her how happy and excited I was today, and she responded, "I have never been excited for anything in my life, except maybe purses."

As the day went by, she cleaned while recovering from her prolonged cold. She asked me to get Micah some pizza.

"Delivery or frozen?" I asked. I could not hear her response, so she became irritated.

"Why are you yelling, honey?" I replied in a flat, mild tone. Instantly, I knew I had lost some control of my positive energy.

Without aggression, she began to explain her frustration, and at that moment, I had a swarming attack of feelings, emotions, and negative energy throughout my body and mind. As I slowly walked to the couch and sat down to breathe, gloomy clouds appeared. The negative energy began to generate dark thoughts. Why am I unable to make my wife happy? Why is she often frustrated? Why does she have this negative energy?

She saw and noticed that my energy and demeanor had changed; she felt terrible for her frustrations and aggression, and apologized. The more she apologized, the quieter I got. I proceeded slowly to lie on the couch without words or emotion. The arched brick wall became my focus as I blankly fixed my gaze. Having been filled with all this energy, I could not identify whether it was negative or positive. The only way to describe what happened next is that my soul left my body.

My mind was hollow. Spirit, energy, and positivity had vanished with a click. Lying there helpless, the evil spirit had taken control of my body and psyche. My entire body was paralyzed—it felt like the dark spirit had restraint over it. There was no energy or motivation to move. Fully aware and conscious of my surroundings, I saw Max looking at me. He started to panic. He began tearing up and immediately came to check on me. With no response from me, he hastily got his mother.

In disbelief and confusion, my wife tried to shake me from the state of paralysis. Max began to cry, and as I watched him, unable to control his emotions, I mustered up the strength to call him over and tell him to breathe and pray for Daddy. I had no idea what else to do or say. I was terrified.

Deeply saddened and hurt, I battled to find the strength to get up and comfort him. That was the worst feeling I had experienced in my life: helpless to help my son. Slowly glancing over at my wife, who wore a look of despair, and with an ominous whisper, I told her, "Tell my mother to come here and pray for me." She hurried to find my mother.

Distraught and frightened, my mother, who we call grandma, proceeded to panic. She could not fathom what her eyes were witnessing, thinking it was health-related. She called my sister Lynn.

Lifeless, spiritless, and soulless, I told them to stop panicking and pray for me. I looked at them through someone else's eyes and felt a body not of my own. My hands and feet were cold and sweaty, so they began to rub ginger and other ointments on me to try to calm me. They ended up calling the ambulance, even though I was opposed to it. The paramedics came and immediately started taking my vital signs.

While I continued to lay there frozen and helpless, embarrassed by the situation, I calmly repeated, "I'm OK. I'm OK."

As I knew, this was a spiritual, unnatural experience and not an illness, dehydration, or anything physical. I was discomposed, afraid, and unable to explain my condition. With an empty stare into my sister's sorrowful eyes, all I could produce was a monotone, "Pray for me. They can't help me." She calmly looked into my eyes with tears and replied, "I know. Big sister knows. I am praying for you."

After all the testing showed that I was physically and internally stable, the paramedics left. I lay back down, once again repeating, "I'm OK. I'm OK."

Still in a vacant, soulless state, I dosed off for ten to fifteen minutes. I woke with the lights off, and as I regained some life, I sat on the couch and began praying to my late mother-in-law, the voice that had guided me on this path.

Everyone finally left, and as I slowly regained strength, I tried my best to explain and describe the unnatural experience to my wife. After a lengthy explanation, I proceeded to the bedroom to check on the children as they slept. I kissed them both and prayed to my mother-in-law on the bed. I prayed again in the shower and a third time on my knees in the bathroom.

I had allowed my wife's energy to affect me negatively, and that allowed the evil spirit, the evil force, to take hold of and control my body. Never again will I allow my weakness to surface, and I will never allow my kids to experience the pain and fear of losing me again.

Now gifted with this abundance of positive energy, I have the strength to identify the negative energy and feedback of others and transfer it to positive energy, not to let it affect me. I know that my experience with the unnatural was authentic. My mother-in-law's voice was real. The sudden revelation and experience with God and the spirit had come full force in those months, and that night was the physical encounter with the evil spirit. The unnatural experience with the evil spirit undoubtedly helped me attain that positive energy.

My wife and children are my life. I'm staying on this path of truth and positivity to become a better person for them. I am now calm, humbled, joyful, and grateful, and I have discovered my journey. Reliving the second part of my life has begun. Strength is within me. My path and journey are my strength.

WELCOMING GRIEF

"We unknowingly desire suffering. Break free of it to allow our attributes to endure the hardships."

With the newfound outlook, I realized all this positive energy prepared me for future adverse events and heartache. Looking back on my past self, I always imagined how I would respond to future tragedies, like a loved one's death. I thought of how I would react and respond to my mother's and wife's deaths, as the dark thoughts resonated within. I would self-pity, hide in a hole, isolate, and indirectly bring attention to myself; that was the only way I knew how to cope with a tragedy and deal with pain and suffering. The new outlook has led me to understand and accept death. To enjoy all of life's beauty: miracles, tragedies, pain, and suffering. Live completely, live well, and live positively regardless of your circumstances.

When a day of tragedy does arrive, I can say with truth that I will no longer live in pain. I will embrace life and treasure those still around, still living: my family, friends, and children. They would still need me to continue living a happy life, free of pain and misery, for I would continue to heavily influence their lives. I don't want to lose sight of what is important in life, as tragedies can happen at any moment.

By living selflessly and not dwelling in our sorrow, we can inspire others to see that happiness and inner peace are attainable despite hardships. Cherish and value the people in our lives who love and support us, while striving to impact their lives positively.

I will teach my children how to cope and adapt to sorrow, heartache, and death, as my wife and I will one day leave this Earth. I will have them continue to live a happy, meaningful, successful life full of positivity and love. I want to live genuinely for my children, long enough to show and teach them to accept life and respond positively. This will be my gift to them.

A longtime friend and client, Kisa, lost her mother, Mrs. Wilhelmina, to cancer a few years back; Mrs. Wilhelmina was also a client—charismatic and full of life. She was struck with stress and pain, and I noticed her drastic weight loss. Her confidence grew with the drastic weight loss and changes in her physique, but the sadness, pain, and stress were dominant. I began to worry secretly and was saddened for her.

I now realize we can be unaware of how our negative or positive energy influences those around us: family, friends, and acquaintances. The more we experience life's traumas, tragedies, and misfortunes, the heavier we carry our burdens. We pick up pain and sorrow on the way, adding to the mountain of burdens that follows us throughout our lives. Internal peace becomes unbearable and difficult to attain as we lose control of our emotions, bodies, and minds. Our minds weaken with every experience of trauma.

Welcome grief, but do not allow it to mold you. We sometimes unknowingly change to a different person and fall victim to the pain and suffering. Lethargy supplants our pain, and anger replaces our compassion. It can eventually manifest in acts of sin, hate, aggression, envy, lust, greed, gluttony, sloth, and pride.

We must not allow our past experiences to dictate our decisions in the future. Let go of the past to shape a better ending. While we accumulate life's traumas, it deteriorates our motivation to live, self-improve, learn, and try new things.

THE IDEA

"Experience this life to its full potential; don't just imagine it."

On Tuesday, August 29, 2023, while my best friend of over twenty years, David, who had just lost his father to a heart attack, was inside the funeral home with his family and the monks, I took his son, Jax, outside in his stroller around the parking lot with my wife. Jax became antsy, so I started to read a passage from my journal on my phone. After I was finished, my wife turned to me with surprise.

"That was poetic," she said. "You're such a philosopher." I was shocked, as I would never consider myself as such.

An idea would blossom. With courage and plenty of verve, the conception of this manuscript had begun. Never in a million years would the idea have crossed my mind; I had never read an entire book in my adult life, let alone author one. If the idea had emerged in the past, I would have needed more determination and perseverance to pursue it. From death, an idea was born.

This journey has taken me to an unimaginable life full of positive energy, motivation, and passion. The courage to proceed with an idea has taken its course. With death all around, I refused to waste any more time.

I was lazy, sleeping my life away, hiding from the struggles and failures. Now I want every second to be used meaningfully. Living a happy life means living well, not long. I embrace what is to come; my path to writing has begun.

Writing this memoir seemed out of reach and beyond comprehension, given my limited intellectual ability. While faith had swaddled my existence, I felt more compelled to learn, self-educate, and become more courageous in this unfamiliar territory.

With absolutely zero knowledge of the book industry, what to do, how to do it, or where to start, I found myself confident that the process would only improve and positively impact my life. Without hesitation or fear, I conjured the courage to take the first steps to pursue the idea the very next morning. I contacted an online book publishing company for the necessary information on how to proceed and create a manuscript.

Faith led me to the publishing company to help me self-publish. An enthusiastic, genuine employee named Ivan helped me tremendously with the process, although his mild, Middle Eastern accent sometimes made him somewhat difficult to understand. With newfound patience and a path, I decided this was my chosen partnership.

The sudden attack of positive energy—overflowing with thoughts and words—made me begin a journal of notes and thoughts on my phone. With eight months of notes, I transferred twenty-four pages worth of thoughts, nine thousand one hundred words total. I began to write in the middle of the night with calm, relaxing, soothing, angelic rhythms to ease the mind, and in the daytime in my head.

I had an epiphany: Death can create new life, new miracles, physically and spiritually, or result in further suffering. With all the recent deaths of close friends and family members that had occurred, life and living with meaning had become a priority.

I accept that misfortunes, internal illness, or death may come at any moment; my current state has been replaced with tranquility and peace. How we respond to death defines us. We always say, "Life is short," but we do not realize what this means until something tragic happens.

CHAPTER EIGHT

THE PATH TO SELF-IMPROVEMENT

THE CHANGES

*"When the mind and spirit are
healthy, the body follows."*

G ROWING UP, I WAS always taught to be unique; I tend
to be different only in manageable areas. My route to
being different is to live against the odds—not to be discouraged—and strive for perfection. I am now not pretending
to be someone I am not. I do not want to be the person I
used to be. I can change overnight.

Realizing my lack of knowledge, I began progressing,
further pursuing enlightenment. Embarking on this
newfound journey, I find myself waking in the middle of
the night, full of energy, ideas, and words. Listening to *Music
of Angels and Archangels*, a slow, soothing, angelic harmony
that my sister Nina found online, helped ease my mind. The
music has allowed abundant, positive energy and thoughts
to burst through my reality. While unable to fall back asleep,
I discovered for the first time that I had been more productive with my time, as I continued drafting this manuscript.

Emerging from an inner passage of self-reflection, I
have utilized time, focused on writing, coaching, faith, and
instructing my boys, Max and Micah, and my godsons,
Evan and Jax, on the values of life—to instill motivation to
become successful in all their endeavors. It is prudent that I

spoil them with knowledge instead of material things. Any form of success is now motivated by thoughts of the children, the boys, and other people's children. The essence of self-improvement is for others rather than just for yourself.

Even the approach to sharing the journey has changed over a fleeting period. Unable to find meaning and purpose in the bountiful positive energy, I knew how to share my journey and path only verbally. At the same time, my reality overflowed with words of love and happiness.

Gifted with the idea of writing this manuscript, it was guided to me by my late mother-in-law, a gift to help contain and equate this wealth of positive energy, to share the words and experiences with loved ones mindfully. Never in my wildest dreams would this mind imagine accompanying this thought.

During my high school days, aside from the family beauty salon business, my first job was as a bookbinder at a publishing company. My days were filled with the routine of binding books, cutting paper, and packaging boxes. Looking back, the idea of writing a book was not remotely possible.

I now realize we can achieve limitless possibilities beyond our current way of thinking if we embrace our full potential.

I continue to recondition my mind and spirit, and this development has positively impacted my health and physical appearance. I no longer have the mindset to work out to look good and desire approval from others. I was conceited, egotistical, selfish, and focused on achieving a toned body with a six-pack and seeking admiration from others. All of this is fueled by negative energy and negative thoughts.

My mental state has changed; I am now working out for my family, health, and mental well-being. My mind has become healthier, and the weight has drastically fallen off in a brief period.

In addition to receiving compliments about my weight loss, I am fully aware of the concerned opinions about it and I am considerate of the worries. I began eating more to try to control the weight loss. The weight has since increased and is manageable.

Rapid weight loss can result from trauma, stress, and tragedy. Likewise, it can result in happiness, fulfillment, and a healthy, productive mind. Physical attributes are the result of a healthy mind.

For years, I suffered from constant back pain. The aching and straining of my lower back would recur every six to eight months, and despite frequent visits to the chiropractor, the relief was only temporary. My unsettled mind and damaged spirit were contributing to the pain. I noticed that my minor health issues gradually disappeared when my mind and soul strengthened.

Coincidentally, I bumped into my chiropractor at our men's Bible study group, where I shared how faith strengthened my spirit and assisted with my absence from his office. He was more than happy to see my improvement and I was grateful for his practice and devotion to faith.

My attire has changed from comfortable athletic name brands to a more tailored, polished, and well-dressed style. This change reflects a more profound shift in my expression and how I present myself to the world.

My diet also became a focus. For over a year, I consumed sea moss for its nutritional value. It is my only vitamin consumption; it contains ninety-two essential vitamins and minerals vital for the body.

With the development of my health, my body has shown less stress and worry. Any successful dietary regimen starts with a robust and healthy mind. I tell myself: healthy mind, healthy spirit, healthy body. I am in the best shape of my life.

I have become more aware of my age and limited lifespan, taking necessary steps to prolong my health and mind. Reserving fifteen to twenty minutes to meditate has a unique way of obtaining and balancing time with my busy new life. Meditation and natural supplements have become daily routines. The practice of spiritual self-healing, along with the sea moss diet, has helped tremendously with my physical well-being.

I also began fasting. The primary purpose of this was originally weight loss—health benefits came second. Frequent headaches, minor aches, and pain have long been absent during my fasts. As my faith deepened, the motivations and justifications for fasting significantly shifted and I switched from a three-day fast to an intermittent one. Fasting became a fad and a trend. I felt the identity had become blurred when the reasons behind the fast became a competition of hours and days, for the objective had veered from losing weight to looking good.

Jesus went into the wilderness and fasted for forty days, proving He was the Son of God. He did so to conquer the flesh, to deny His natural desires and temptations from Satan. The purpose of a fast is to give us spiritual strength through prayers and meditation and devote ourselves to seeking God. If we can conquer hunger, we can control our being.

The discovery of a fast depicted in the Bible further solidified my views of where the modern path of fasting was headed—in the opposite direction of health and spiritual aspects. Even a biblical topic such as fasting had become spiritual warfare. It seems as though Satan has hijacked the practice of fasting, too.

My search for spiritual healing and self-care developed from a daily fasting practice—where I ate only once per day—to a lifestyle. The shift in intention transcended me to a closer, more profound daily spiritual connection with God. Whenever I need to delve into a deep connection with God, I tackle a multi-day fast.

While my physical and mental transformation continued to develop, it transpired a shift from my vainness. I have been wearing contacts since high school and I hated glasses. Why? My perception of wearing glasses is that they make me feel uncomfortable, less confident, and dorky. I do not look good in glasses. I conjure up excuses and lies not to wear glasses: I play sports, they fit weirdly, and they are heavy.

I now realize why my mind and body prefer glasses over contacts. My frame of mind has become more confident, positive, loving life, and loving myself. The contacts have been giving me trouble lately. Drying up constantly; I think it's the hot weather. I feel less confident as I keep squinting like I have some sort of condition. I now wear glasses. They do not feel heavy and fit perfectly, resulting in a healthy mind. My brain has told my body that wearing contacts is uncomfortable and glasses are perfect. The change reflected the inner transformation I have been experiencing.

While our physical abilities may be limited, our minds are not. Rewire your brain so that it possesses unlimited possibilities.

PROGRESS IN LIVING WELL

*"Identifying faults in your happiness begins
with self-reflection and self-improvement."*

I continue to listen to calm, angelic harmony every morning before the gym, as a source of meditation. It guides me through the day to withhold any anger or aggressive emotion that may arise, resulting in a drastic change in my temperament in recent months.

When anger is rising, take deep breaths and focus on positive thoughts. Pause and stretch the feelings to allow time to settle in. Avoid engaging in irrational behavior. Our minds become unclouded as the emotions begin to withdraw and disappear.

We try to conquer authority by countering someone's anger and aggression with our own. Suppressing anger, frustration, and aggression with time can help restrain verbal abuse and, sometimes, physical abuse. Instead of projecting your emotions verbally, discipline yourself to delay and hold on to your feelings to give yourself time to think clearly before reacting.

Emotions typically last only sixty to ninety seconds. Knowing this can help us gain better control over our emotions and behaviors. If you are unable to control your emotions, neither extreme excitement and lust nor sadness and hatred can be contained. Delaying the emotions is the secret to controlling anger.

These methods have helped me tremendously in restricting anger and aggression in everyday situations. My mind used to be clouded with stress, worry, and anger, but once I learned how to control the emotions, sound judgments were achievable when those emotions arose. Now, the words and actions of others do not plague my emotions and thoughts or control my behavior. Managing my feelings has also helped me overcome anxiety.

I have chosen to conquer my emotions, not let them dictate my behavior, in the long term to ensure that anger does not govern my thoughts and actions. These feelings are temporary and do not shape one's character, nor should they run wild.

Minor changes in me began to occur during the self-improvement. I frequently craved new words and spent hours with online dictionaries and thesauruses to help expand my vocabulary and mind. My memory has improved; it was nonexistent before. Reading the dictionary and Bible has helped stimulate my brain and elevate my memory.

My speech has shifted to a calmer, softer, slower tone. Words now have different meanings, as I have become more aware of finding meaningful and impactful words to use, changing the vocabulary and language in my mind from negative to positive every moment. Identifying and separating negative and positive words eliminates any phrase with negative connotations. I have replaced them with loving, meaningful words to describe the path, truth, and thoughts. I am mindful of words, proof that humbleness is an achievable virtue.

Food has become even more enjoyable with Cindy, my extensive family's chef, with her traditional yet exquisite cooking touch. As everything began to taste delightful, I asked my wife to stop requesting feedback and critiques of her cooking. Every lunch and dinner is utterly unique and delicious.

Past relationships and experiences taught me to lie with my cooking critiques. The avoidance of inflicting hurt and disappointment was no longer the reason. Truth and honesty had outweighed the fear of disappointment.

My new love for fruit and vegetables has increased compared to being a carnivore. The words "eat your fruits and vegetables" became my motto. I am gradually changing my old, unshakable ways. I'm beginning to enjoy the little things, and all aspects of life are blissful and gratifying.

While I progressed a step closer to where I wanted to be, I made the clear, sound decision to file bankruptcy rather than worrying about finances. I had to take steps to escape this negative situation. Once the filing is completed in nine months, I thought, my credit will improve, giving way to a fresh, clean slate.

As the process began, I focused on the stress and worry. Upon meeting the lawyer, Mrs. Shaffer, and her secretary, Mrs. Moffat, they greeted me with kindness and without judgment—they were a breath of fresh air. A blessing was sent to guide me as they were referred to me by my late, close friend and CPA, Mrs. Veronica. Their genuineness and generosity dampened the worries and stress. They succeeded in making the experience bearable and comforting.

This experience gave me confidence in my relationships and future relations. I felt that I was sufficiently competent to control myself and that I could develop any relationship: my wife, family, friends, strangers, and even those who don't like me.

READING MY FIRST BOOK AS AN ADULT

*"I never imagined replacing my
phone with a book."*

I have noticed that I've been relatively inactive and nonexistent on social media lately—the thirst to self-entertain through those forms is a futile use of my time. I have also cut back on online engagement of government and world issues. Engaging in political debates only fuels self-indulgence and desire for attention, especially as the negative encounters increase. I have begun to focus on more meaningful friendships through real-life interactions and conversations, with the passion and motivation to make every human encounter a more positive, worthwhile experience. The joyous reward is the feeling of liberation from the influence of social media.

This morning, there was a book on the table that Jonathan, an amazingly wise and successful dentist, had sent me. I had compared and competed with him internally, by finding his flaws to elevate myself above his financial superiority. Society's standards of success have conditioned me to feel inferior compared to others.

I falsely valued my strengths in other areas to compensate for my lack of financial achievements, resulting in the wicked thought that I was better than him in that regard. Jonathan forgave me when I confessed and pleaded with gratitude and admiration for his forgiveness. This confession helped release the burdens of envy and jealousy.

The first book I read as an adult, given to me by Jonathan, is about Seneca, one of the great philosophers of his time and an advisor to Emperor Nero. I began and proceeded to the end of the first paragraph. A rush of feelings and emotions entered my body. An attack of words rushed through my brain. I had to put the book down, as my mind began to generate constant thoughts.

Consumed, I wrote them down. My vocabulary was limited, and so was my intellect. I tried my best to translate the feelings into words, thinking at this rate it would take me decades to finish reading the book.

Why had I never read a book, wanted to read, or improve myself? Why did I need to read or find other means to better myself? Questioning my inability to understand books and words and my boredom, I could learn through other, more entertaining means. I would instead read social media content that gave me immediate satisfaction and gratification.

Social media interaction, whether negative or positive, fed into my false sense of knowledge and wisdom. It added unsound confidence to my pride, and I felt aloft and better than others. I was unaware of this while lying to myself that I didn't lack knowledge.

The new passion to self-improve has long outweighed the urge to self-entertain; this lifestyle will overcome any trend.

QUELL YOUR FEARS AND CONQUER YOURSELF

*"Focus on our weaknesses, not
only on our strengths."*

There was a moment of weakness. An inadequate, self-pity feeling fostered the thought of using Artificial Intelligence (AI) to help write this manuscript once the energy had subsided. Contemplating for an hour in my vehicle in front of the gym, the idea of using AI would revert to my old self. Staring at multiple AI applications, I thought, I am cheating myself and others. It would have me pretend and perceive to be an adept writer without the work. I would cheat myself of the process—of an education. I will not allow my old self and old ways to resurface.

Allowing technology to take over would rob me of that experience. Instead, go through the process of learning and be genuine. If we allow technology to hijack our authenticity, we start to lose part of ourselves. Let us find ways to preserve our humanity and imagination as we learn to coexist with the emergence of artificial intelligence.

Believing in myself has provided the necessary drive to follow through with the whole writing process. Especially given my lack of knowledge when comparing my entry-level writing ability to that of others with higher skills and education, the sentiment has not deviated from the passion to complete this book. Failure will always be the result if we do not genuinely believe in our actions.

How do we get from point A to B in terms of writing experience? Our minds tend to skip embracing the process and focus directly on the difficulty of the results—and we become fearful of the hard work. The negative thoughts had once scared me into thinking my writing was not good enough.

As I have come to learn, true writing is the catalyst for the start of good writing. The feeling of incompetency in writing knowledge was short-lived, understanding there was a time when experienced writers were once in my shoes. Do not let your mind veer off to focus on the negative. Self-doubt can consume you and is the enemy's influence. Courage is the absence of fear and worry. Believe and remain optimistic about success. Be true to yourself.

As the busy holiday season approached, I was reluctant to take a small break from the manuscript. I found myself buried in devices as I continued to write on my phone. Thus, realizing the repetitive nature of using devices and their convenience, I rediscovered the beauty of writing in my journal. Journaling has been an essential tool for enhancing my creativity, as it has helped me to improve my sub-par memory by recording my thoughts and ideas. Moreover, it has also provided a calming and comforting influence during busy times.

I will become a writer.

I will complete this book.

No matter what.

Faith and discernment in the plan allowed me to focus on all aspects of my life, not only areas where I have strengths. When living only for myself, I could control some areas that required all my energy, whereas I had failed in every other area.

I focused only on my strengths, which yielded confidence. The fears of my vulnerability supplanted the weaknesses.

Often, we tend to applaud and focus on our strengths and ignore our weaknesses because we fear confronting the shortcomings in certain aspects of our lives where we lack confidence. We avoid making complex life changes that require hard work and determination and settle for easy, achievable tasks—our lives become one-dimensional. Things that are easy to achieve do not bring prolonged happiness, which creates an excuse to accept their normality in our daily lives. We can challenge ourselves and appreciate the difficulties of attaining difficult feats, as they will bring us lasting satisfaction and fulfillment. We can be comfortable with our strengths; we can also be uncomfortable but conquer our weaknesses.

Acquiring and accessing knowledge is relatively easy; it is pervasive and available. However, obtaining wisdom can be challenging and may seem unattainable at times. While we may gain knowledge in specific areas, we must often remember to improve in other areas. With knowledge, we build confidence to tackle new challenges and comprehend further, but we may sometimes shy away from unfamiliar territory.

Seeking education is more than just finishing a four-year college degree. However, a college education is a stepping stone to building a foundation of discipline and learning how to procure information. It is the blueprint for training your mind and disciplining your life to complete an objective. Find the desire and motivation to educate yourself and hunger to be better.

Understanding the process of gaining knowledge and retaining information is more valuable than the outcome. Find the determination to receive all the information you can get to help you succeed in life. The challenging part is executing and applying the knowledge to our lives. We were taught fundamental life values as a child and to attain knowledge throughout our lives; still, we seldom implement the simplest values.

The experience of passionately attacking and pursuing an idea I previously had no interest in has left me in awe of the power of determination and perseverance. The courage to pursue is less of a feeling and more of being in a state of absence of fear and worry. Imagine the endless possibilities that would be available channeling the same energy into pursuing any dream. The thought of it is filled with excitement and motivation to strive relentlessly toward an objective. Fear and worry are no longer a nuisance. I tell myself that success is the process, not just the outcome.

I have trained my mind to not just set goals but achievements, as goals can be limiting and sometimes lead to disappointment. Replace goals with tasks and objectives; they can be added to. Even when we do everything right, external factors beyond our control, such as natural disasters, sudden changes in circumstances, or other people's actions, can hinder our abilities and progress. Failing to reach our goals can deter our motivation. This approach allows us to move forward at our own pace and gives us the flexibility to adjust plans when necessary. Instead of focusing on a specific outcome, this approach encourages us to concentrate on the process of achieving objectives and helps us stay motivated and engaged. Work hard until your idol becomes your rival.

The sudden motivation to live, enjoy life, and stay in the present moment has been overwhelming. I am grateful for living, for my mistakes, for experiencing failures many times, and for the light bestowed upon me. The discovery of kindness and mindfulness has been vital to my mental well-being. Happiness appears more than when I was financially comfortable.

Reminiscing on happy memories has intensified this feeling of enjoyment. I want to achieve a genuine smile of joy and not pretend or be perceived as happy. I never smiled in pictures. The lack of confidence, even in a smile, can describe one's internal character. The genuine smile of life has replaced the silly one.

Every decision, every course of action, and recent profound experiences have brought me to this moment. I continue to live honestly and truthfully because it aids in generating positive thoughts—and the outcomes have continued to lead me on the road of faith.

WISE WORDS OF PROVERBS

> *"Through the power of repetition, we can recondition our minds with daily affirmations and words of Proverbs."*

The words of wisdom in Proverbs are plain and straightforward yet difficult to enact and apply; we simply ignore, forget, and devalue them. Steve, the husband of my longtime client Maret, slowly walks toward my table and hands me a yellow sticky note. It reads: "Read one chapter of Proverbs per day, corresponding to each day of the month, and repeat every month." Oh, what a lovely gesture, I thought.

Interested and somewhat ecstatic, I eagerly applied the routine the following morning. Amazed by Proverbs' comprehensible language and meanings, I texted Maret with excitement and gratitude.

This has been one of the most valuable gifts I have been blessed with—a treasure that will be cherished and adopted forever. A small gesture of faith resulted in an impactful deed. When evil spirits and persistent negative thoughts have invaded, the discipline of returning to Proverbs reminded me to pursue wisdom—turning to the Scriptures. If you truly believe in the information you receive, it will not feel imposed upon you.

Our minds constantly absorb information and filter it through our beliefs and perspectives. Unfortunately, this means we are often bombarded with negative thoughts and emotions. Reconditioning our minds is similar to how we were taught values and morals as children. We were constantly reminded of the importance of honesty, respect, and kindness until these values became ingrained in our minds and behaviors. In the same way, by repeating positive affirmations and life reminders, we can shape our minds and instill new values, positive thoughts, and belief in ourselves, helping us overcome negative self-talk. Faith and words of wisdom healed my body and psyche.

WHERE DO OUR MORALS COME FROM?

"Live not just to be in existence but to exist graciously and with full intent."

The enemy influenced my first thought of my increasingly noticeable gray hairs. For a split second, vain came alive, as I read that gray hair is a sign of wisdom. I quickly shifted my mindset toward embracing the gray hair as a symbol of wisdom. We can interpret these simple situations in so many ways, depending on the development of our understanding and the stages in our lives. Embrace life, embrace the changes, embrace the passage of time.

I have been on the routine of Proverbs for four months now, and recently Proverbs 8:12-36 caught my attention. It made me think about how we define good and bad judgments and where our morals come from. I also wondered how our concept of morality has changed throughout human history.

While reading the passage, the idea of vengeance crossed my mind. Like many people, I have imagined taking ultimate vengeance if someone I love was ever harmed. However, I also know that throughout history, stories depicting vengeance as immoral have slowly transitioned to honorable and necessary acts. We often commit acts of vengeance in the name of respect and justice, and the influence of news and movies has shifted to glorifying vengeance as entertainment.

On the other hand, adultery has been widely accepted as a societal norm, even though we know deep down that it's an immoral act. Embedded in us, our intense emotions of protectiveness and jealousy exist to prevent infidelity; we can understand these emotions' underlying causes and recognize when they are becoming destructive. However, social constructs and cultural norms have allowed these acts to be overlooked. Evidently, our flawed modern society has greatly influenced the evolution of our moral compass and values.

Through the Scriptures and my relationship with Christ, I have gained a better understanding of my morals and strengths. I am determined to have complete control over every aspect of myself, including my emotions, thoughts, and spirit, not just my physical self. I trust God to guide me in living mindfully in a world that's often cursed.

Life is full of contradictions, including this book. That is the beauty of it.

CHAPTER NINE

MY INTERPRETATION

THERE IS ONE GOD

"The Bible tells the story of God's unfailing love for all of humanity, his children, conveyed through various accounts with various perspectives, experiences, and messages."

CHRISTIANITY, OTHER RELIGIONS, AND nonreligious perspectives are merely our righteous interpretations of moral living. No one can tell me my beliefs are wrong, and I cannot say the same to them. However, we can change our perspective.

I have heard both positive and negative stories about religion and the church. But somehow, I allowed the terrible stories and negative experiences to overshadow the church's teachings, meanings, and positive aspects. The negative stories have eclipsed the positive ones. This perspective distanced me from all religions—the need to question faith and the church when others had represented it poorly. I looked only for its flaws.

We become bored and feel uneducated about our interest in religion and faith. Our beliefs are influenced to falsely feel that having faith is against humanity, against human rights, and forcing oneself to think a certain way.

I resolved that religion and the church are not flawed themselves; rather, imperfect humans are the faulty components.

The bad should never outweigh the good. I am learning that humans, including myself, are born pure at heart but can easily be influenced by the forces of evil. I now live with empathy and look for the positive aspects in others, the church, and religion.

Jesus, with divine peace, achieved ultimate patience and discernment of the plan. He knew he could not change the world immediately and adapted to that understanding with his sacrifice. His words and teachings would reach individuals like me—thousands of years later.

The purpose of sharing the Scriptures, words, and messages with others is not to force understanding or make others change their lives but to encourage and give hope to those currently on the path. Those who have already understood or are receptive, or want to seek change, will continue to pursue it. The Bible will always be there waiting.

We will know when to share our faith and encouragement mindfully. These experiences, words, and messages will also be waiting.

If Jesus were present here today, would we follow him? Or would judgment get the best of us and would we judge him? Would we look for his flaws, condemn him, or acknowledge what his sinless life symbolizes and stands for?

Foreseeing his disciples' betrayal, with different motives, responses, and outcomes, Jesus had already forgiven them and allowed the betrayal to happen, fulfilling God's plan. With spiritual discernment and prayers, Jesus attained inner peace, remained peaceful, and accepted his fate. He allowed judgment from others to reign, ultimately causing his death.

Jesus could have easily escaped death. But he led by example, sacrificing his sinless life to guide us, show us the way of life, and pass down the message. He sacrificed his life to rinse away our sins, for we have the power and the choice not to sin, and be free from eternal death.

On the cross, Jesus exposed his vulnerability and cried out to his Father, asking Him to forgive those who condemned him to death. Despite the pain and hatred inflicted upon him, Jesus chose to forgive them. Though physically at his weakest, he demonstrated mental strength, filled with love and compassion. He did not blame or hate but showed empathy, the ultimate power of forgiveness, and the will of God—he chose to love.

Even a perfect soul can be condemned, as others judge and fear what they do not understand and cannot achieve themselves. We dismiss what Jesus' ideal life symbolizes and look for his flaws, pure judgment on our part. Let us not overlook the message and meaning of his perfect soul and allow the power of judgment to repeat the same story. Instead, we can follow with an open heart and mind.

The valid message behind Jesus' crucifixion is that a perfect being can coexist in a sinful world and achieve absolute forgiveness in human form. I, too, have finally forgiven those who committed such acts of sin influenced by the enemy, our sinful nature. Judgment of others is a sin to me.

The focus is on striving to live a sinless life. The teachings are that only our Lord is perfect and sinless—we are not and will never be capable of achieving such a thing. This can stray us from the path and demotivate us from striving toward righteousness. We embody sin as expected and cannot live without it.

Though sin is part of life, we can pursue a righteous path. Is that not what the Scriptures and stories teach? To follow the Lord, follow him on the journey to heaven. To live well with love, kindness, compassion, forgiveness, and positivity.

We humans are capable of acts such as forgiveness, accepting life, the good and the bad, and accepting the consequences of free will. Our savior unveiled the path to heaven for our souls to live on for eternity.

I believe that every living being is the culmination of past lives who have lived worthy of heaven. We exist as continuous souls traversing through heaven—the eternal life cycle. How we live in this life, our choices, our actions, and how we treat others determines our ongoing path to heaven. Only we can truly assess and honestly ask ourselves if we will reach paradise in the afterlife again.

NO LONGER WORSHIPPING MYSELF

> *"I do not fear death; I fear the Lord,*
> *as He is the moral value of life."*

These thoughts and words are not from me but from the spirit. As abundant beings, we have the innate purpose of worshipping God by design.

Looking back, my lack of interest in faith was fueled by pride, which played a part in the rejection of God. I went against the plan and worshipped myself or nothing at all. Sinning was easy. I had utilized my human imperfections to justify my continued wrongdoing.

However, I am now vigilantly pursuing humility. I have abandoned worshiping myself and am committed to embracing a more humble and spiritual way of life. God is something you worship other than yourself. God was and is.

My God is good and evil. Though this is not a new concept, I have concluded and embraced this reality. According to my faith, God is the source and is responsible for all things; light and darkness, good and bad, are the will of God. He is infinite and eternal—a spirit with no beginning and no end. Only matter has a beginning and end.

Scripture teaches us that God "creates evil" but does not commit evil or approve of sin. Yet, His sovereignty allows evil to happen while directing and using it for good purposes. The "D" was a good guy who became the lord of "darkness," while sinners can become saints. God is dualistic and creates all opposites: peace and war, men and women, love and hate, and so forth. This translates to the concept of good and evil co-existing. My failure to understand this concept also added to my disinterest in God. Why would anyone worship a God that creates evil and suffering? This is the will and plan, finding the balance of free will.

Good and evil occupy my mind simultaneously. Creating life and reproduction are the effects of God, as He is life and light, the cause of everything, beyond our reality. The "D" is time, darkness, and death. The idea of life on Earth is to procreate and live forever in peace. We can achieve eternity once we live together peacefully as one human race.

Inherently, we are neither good nor bad. With free will, we can actively choose to be influenced by positive or negative forces, God or Satan.

I now understand why some people feel the necessity to thank God first and foremost. Those words capture feelings of embarrassment and vulnerability. I had not placed God first above all else. Fear of the Lord—to fear

God. Unselfishly, we can give our lives to God, submit to a higher deity, and ascend beyond ourselves.

Does a spirit constitute only being inside the universe, or can it exist outside? The understanding is that God is the spirit of the universe, inside and out. Creation itself is brought into existence by a creator, incomprehensible beyond our knowledge.

There are things science cannot answer. Belief is not knowing. I believe in something that science may or may not prove. Science cannot prove or tell what happened before the Big Bang thirteen billion years ago. Science cannot disprove that there is a God, which leads to possibilities. Why do we believe that something like the Big Bang can form from nothing but not God? That is God.

If the Big Bang was the cause of everything, what caused and created the Big Bang? If God was the cause of everything, what caused and created God?

Time, with its dual nature, can heal all things, yet it can also sow doubt. It carries a sense of unreality to the present, transforming history into myth and stories into fantasies.

I choose to believe in God. You can only believe in what lies beyond your understanding. The universe is as limitless as every mind and limited to the duration of a mind's life. We can live with God in this reality, and our spirit will be with Him when human life ends. We can live without God, and we will not be with Him in the afterlife.

Spirituality is the pursuit of a connection with a higher power without necessarily using religious titles or labels— God without the title. Some seek God and some seek spiritual enlightenment to find purpose and motivation. However, I think it's essential that we fully grasp ourselves before we go beyond the moral teachings of any religion, including Christianity, to gain a deeper cognition of our spirituality.

When we delve deeper into these subjects, we may become more rigid in our beliefs and isolate ourselves from others who have different perspectives. Rather than getting distracted by these differences, we should focus on living our lives with mindfulness and humility while striving to find balance in everything we do.

We were born physically imperfect in size and shape. But our minds were born pure of greed, pride, lust, envy, gluttony, wrath, and sloth; our minds were born perfect.

As we enter the world, our imperfect body (negative energy, evil spirit) coincides with an ideal mind (positive energy, God); we develop and allow life to take hold as we experience all the beauty and love. We also begin to experience all the misfortunes and tragedies as we are cursed. Humans are hardwired to absorb all the good and evil of the world.

While the foundation of faith solidifies, it has taught mindfulness of all religions—mindful of God's gift of free will, free to choose, free to think. Mindfulness practice led to most religions teaching similar life values and lessons to bring about a peaceful, meaningful life. Beyond that, we tend to dissociate the similarities and veer toward individual beliefs.

Continuing to expand my knowledge and understanding of the world around me and deciphering the meanings has been increasingly clear. It has become obvious that these experiences have been written about and depicted in the book of Romans, no matter how unique or unusual, even in modern times.

Eager to learn more, I immediately turned to Romans, hoping for answers and a deeper understanding of the changes. My curiosity remained steadfast, and I was driven to uncover the hidden answers and truths beneath the surface of everyday existence.

My outlook on life further changed when I no longer worshipped myself and stopped judging others. It was not until then that I finally understood the meaning of the fourteenth chapter of the book of Romans. The difference was that I searched and found those words on my own. They were not forced upon me, like in the past; I sought them. If I had come across them in the past, they would have been overlooked and ignored, and I would continue to live with judgment.

Romans 14 can be interpreted to focus on peace and avoid quarrels. The main component is to not judge one another. Welcome the weak. For a devout Christian, having the freedom to exercise an action does not make it acceptable. The foremost duty is to prevent actions that could lead a fellow believer, who may be weaker in their faith, to stumble. If an individual's conscience deems something impure to the extent that it cannot permit them to partake, it is indeed considered impure for that individual. In this scenario, it is morally impermissible to go against their conscience. Doing so would constitute a sin. Stricter Christians can easily judge others; even so, we should not pass judgment. This underscores the individual responsibility and empowerment that comes with our personal faith and conscience.

It is vital to comprehend that those with stricter convictions, referred to as "weaker" faith Christians by Paul, should not impose their restrictions on other believers. The weak are the ones who judge other Christians, even though they live a Christian life and see themselves as the stronger ones. Believing something to be a sin for oneself does not imply that it is automatically a sin for others. Instead of contempt for those who do not share a nonessential belief, we can strive to mindfully understand and accept that anyone who acts against their conscience is engaging in sinful behavior. The strong in faith can bear with those who are weak in the conscience of faith.

LIMITLESS POSSIBILITIES OF FREE WILL

"Heaven is within me."

God created us with the most powerful ability in life, the most desirable and magical feeling: creating life. The most incredible feeling carries the greatest responsibility. We are barely a fraction of time—procreation is the only way to keep up with time. As the enemy befriends us, our minds are clouded with negativity and opposing morals of Jesus to interrupt procreation. What happens when we slow down our procreation? The long-term effect is our extinction.

This faith concedes that we are created to reproduce and exceed beyond this world—to find balance. The Bible teaches that we have eternal life and that our souls and certain aspects of ourselves are passed down to our offspring for generations, creating strong connections and bonds between parents and their children. We may pass down knowledge and wisdom from generation to generation to live in harmony—the fight against time.

We are created with a free mind and free will to unlock our minds without limitations, evolve, progress, reproduce, and live forever as intelligent species in an infinite universe. Only a free mind can progress unlimitedly (to think freely without limits). As time passes, fiction slowly becomes a reality. However, free will enables both good and evil to exist.

Our ability to live forever comes with conditions. The curse of a free mind and free will is that it welcomes and opens the door to evil. The balance of life is light and life, darkness and death, yin and yang. Living peacefully among each other is the path to endure life's misfortunes, the way to overcome evil.

The belief is that human life and our future have been pre-recorded and predetermined, but we interpret the same experiences differently. This suggests that God has a plan for us, comprising positive and negative experiences we will encounter throughout our lives. Whether it is a joyous occasion or a difficult challenge, everything that happens in our lives is a stepping stone toward fulfilling God's plan for all of us.

No one desires hell. We all would choose heaven. How do we achieve that, or do we even know where to start? Every sin committed has consequences. Whether significant or insignificant, karma has a way of showing itself.

What is heaven? How do we describe it? My interpretation of heaven is that it is perfect—spiritually. It is not necessarily a place but a state of mind—perfect in every way—living with perfect thoughts, speech, and actions. The idea becomes unachievable as we experience life's disasters and tragedies.

The teachings show that Jesus is heaven. God is within me and within us to guide a life free of sin with compassion, empathy, and forgiveness—an attainable calmness.

Upon discovering Christianity and spirituality simultaneously, I encountered a slight separation between the two through various interactions; they are the same. Whether you are on a spiritual enlightenment or the path of faith, it is the same journey.

Seeking both motivates me to live better for myself and others—achieving inner peace, patience, happiness, truthfulness, kindness, and self-control. I want to preserve the motivation to live well, live healthy, and live with love. Spirituality will not separate me from God, nor will faith distance spirituality.

Intertwining experiences with faith and spirituality have led to this journey of self-growth and unlimited self-discovery to achieve the same principles of better living. Born anew, my spirit has been cleansed, free from sin. I can now live a spirit-filled life, free from the temptations of the flesh. By experiencing heaven on Earth, one can reach heaven in the afterlife. My path to heaven is truth, love, righteousness, and peace.

CREATING MEANINGFUL FRIENDSHIPS

CHAPTER TEN

MEANINGFUL RELATIONSHIPS

CREATING MEANINGFUL FRIENDSHIPS

*"Creating meaningful friendships
is the key to a happy life."*

EVERY MORNING, AFTER DROPPING the kids off at school, I looked forward to seeing Pastor Sylvester (Sly) as I entered the gym where he had worked as an employee for years. I have been a member since the gym opened and, for a long time, never noticed or appreciated Pastor Sly's presence. Full of life, energy, positivity, and always with a smile, he navigated through the gym with his love and passion for conversations.

Having finally crossed paths, we became good friends while sharing our journeys and experiences. With a background in ministry, Pastor Sly hesitated to voice his practice in a workplace environment, as some may not be receptive to his words. Yet he continues to pursue sharing his ministry with others. With the spirit of God, one day he openly shared his faith with me. We bonded over our spirituality, and his positive energy edified my journey. Pastor Sly has been my motivation to kick start the day with a smile.

Would you have the tenacity and willingness to befriend someone who has an entirely different lifestyle or values than you, like a preacher or minister? Would you compare and judge yourself or judge them instead?

I used to be scared and timid around preachers, ministers, and monks, afraid they may judge me and my life choices. In their presence, my character and behavior would alter to what I thought was acceptable and, I believed, consciously righteous. However, this facade would crumble in solitude, and I would violate those convictions.

Befriending those with high morals was never a thought. I would naturally surround myself with others who had similar lifestyles. With my feelings of judgment receding, the encounters and friendships with preachers and ministers have been on the rise. Their presence and words no longer bear judgment.

EGO HAS NO PLACE AMONG FRIENDS

"Remove ego and allow compassion to take hold, and we can transform any relationship into a meaningful and everlasting one."

Ego and arrogance closed my eyes to the thought of being the nucleus of my family and extended family and friends. If I were ever to leave or move away, their relationship with each other would falter—especially my two best friends, whom I call my brother and sister, David and his wife, Angela. I was self-centered in thinking that if I move, their relationship would drastically change for the worse.

My wife, David, and Angela are drinking buddies, as we spend a lot of time together, eating and hanging out. I thought our time together would help them not focus on their problems. I was wrong. David and Angela are two amazing people with stunningly different virtues. Only they can create a happy, healthy relationship, not me. The negative energy and a poisonous way of thinking generated that.

I have to let go of my ego and not interfere with their lives. At some point in our lives, we encounter situations where we must come to terms with letting go. This may involve releasing our attachment to someone we love and prioritizing the driving positive forces of love and goodwill. Whether it is a favorable or unfavorable situation, we can make mindful judgments with our hearts.

Persuaded by pride and vanity, I realized how terribly I had been treating a longtime friend, Mitchell. I always thought I was superior to him in every way: education, appearance, relationships, and finances. I thought and treated him like he was one of the children, one of the nephews, as he was seven years younger than me. Jokes toward him at times were harsh, degrading, and simultaneously hilarious (to me, at least). Bashing him entertained our friends.

The unsympathetic mind manifested the notion of pretending Mitchell was an adopted nephew. Jokes about adopting him continued. He eventually became part of the family—not as a friend or an equal but someone I pitied and wanted to care for. I felt he had a lower financial status and limited intellectual abilities. Looking back, I rarely conversed or was present around him whenever he came for family functions, secretly casting a disdainful glare upon my friend.

Continuing this path of truth and forgiveness, I confessed and asked Mitchell for forgiveness for how I had treated him over the years. He had no sense of ill will toward me or how terrible I had been treating him. He happily forgave.

Presently, as I am filled with love, all the dark energy for one of my best friends has vanished. The perception of him has changed with love and empathy. He is my equal, my friend, my brother, and I have been treating him as such. In reality, I look up to Mitchell for being responsible with his finances, his non-addictive character traits, and his loyalty. Degrading jokes have been tamed. We have become closer and have matching unicorn tattoos.

The tattoo was a regrettably made fantasy football bet before the significant life change. I remember being so confident in my skills that I made the bet without thinking twice. However, initially, there was some resistance to following through with the bet, as I had no interest in tattoos. The thought of having a permanent unicorn tattoo was not very appealing to me.

While going through the changes, I quickly shifted to honoring my word and embracing the unicorn I named "Cheeks," located on my right bottom. The day I got the tattoo was filled with anticipation and excitement, no regret or uneasiness. It serves as a testament to the integrity and importance of keeping one's word—the consistency of becoming a good person.

Mitchell and I have bonded through fantasy football with five other close friends: Shawn, Ross, Man, Chris, and my nephew Kelvin. Always competitive with each other, we bash and talk trash, as this is what guys do. This is the first year Mitchell and I became teammates and agreed to have a team side bet with the other four.

I continue playing fantasy football to balance my relationships with my friends. My friends are true happiness, not fantasy football; the struggle with this addiction is no more. With my newfound positivity, Mitchell and I are soulmates. He is my best friend, family, and brother. Our friendship will last for eternity.

The wish for Michael, our state representative, to be part of my fantasy football league has finally come true, as I had asked his wife, Haley, for years to tell him to join my league. I was thrilled when I received the news. I was honored and humbled to discover Michael's nervousness and excitement while he prepared for our draft, as politicians are perceived as intimidating and professional.

Michael is not only a politician but a father and husband and he is humble and down-to-earth. As we prepare for our fantasy draft, we briefly forget world issues and conflicts and enjoy the small things in life that balance us.

At times, we are influenced by the dark, evil spirit to judge friends and family unfavorably. We lose ourselves to vainglory, ego, arrogance, and pride. We forget to love and open our hearts.

We have to forgive ourselves for our negative thoughts and hatred. Regardless of any situation, it is always possible to follow the path leading to inner peace and tranquility. Instead of reacting with anger or hatred toward those who hurt us, we should try to understand them, show empathy, and look for their positive aspects.

Some may struggle and be incapable of letting go, over-looking, or forgiving when their boundaries are met, while some can go beyond. Does this make them wrong for their inability to go beyond their feelings? There is no right or wrong. With discipline, discover the unlimited possibilities we, as humans, are capable of.

When like-minded individuals surround us, the work and influence are relatively easy. The real challenge is the stray sheep. Guiding them back in a positive direction may be diffi-cult. However, we can make an effort to seek out and support these individuals who have lost their way. The influence of the lost sheep can leave a significantly higher imprint on others.

The day may come when our kindness and compassion move them; they may see their path. Forgiveness can help us heal and grow, transforming even the most toxic relationships into positive ones.

ADAPTING TO ONE'S CHARACTER

"This undying love will never perish;
even death will not do us part."

My wife's beauty, selflessness, caring nature, and incomprehensible understanding captivated me, and I knew she was the one for me. Despite having nothing in common, we balance each other, and she is my soulmate. She helped me escape my darkness and reveal my faith. And I was sent to help her uncover her light.

On July Fourth, we were driving back to the house of our friends Sara and Joshua from a movie about child sex trafficking to spend the holiday together. I began to share my passionate thoughts about the film. In the middle of a deep thought, my wife interrupted to inform me we were about to miss a turn.

Blood began rushing through my body. Emotions intensified with anger as I garnered the mental fortitude to stay quiet and calm—the method of delaying anger. With a slight moment of weakness, a low grunt emitted from my throat as I tried to contain the emotions. My wife felt offended and said a multitude of aggressive, defensive words.

At that moment, I knew I had made a mistake. I stayed quiet momentarily to delay the anger, then, calmly but firmly, asked her to please allow me to talk: "I was wrong. That was my fault. I'm sorry I grunted."

She continued to defend herself for interrupting, and said my grunt made her feel like a terrible human being. I continued apologizing and explained my methods of controlling my emotions.

"Please stop talking. Please do not feel bad. It's my fault." I softly spoke the words. "I will try to control my emotions better next time. Please be patient with me as I'm still a work in progress."

My wife slowly withdrew her aggression and apologized for being defensive.

"There's no need to apologize. That was my fault," I pleaded. "I know you meant no harm and that you didn't purposefully interrupt me."

I continued to explain to her that I knew who she was—that is, who she had been for the last eighteen years I had known her.

She can change subjects simultaneously, genuinely switching back and paying full attention to the current subject. That is her amazingly unique character—it took me years to realize this when I eventually removed the ego from my spirit. We both calmly and repeatedly apologized to each other. All of this transpired within a twenty-minute drive.

As we entered the house, our feelings simmered and slowly disappeared and we acted like nothing happened. We had a blast as she drank and mingled throughout the home and we enjoyed the rest of our July Fourth with an amazing fifteen-minute firework show, compliments of Joshua. If I had lost control of my emotions in the car, the situation would have ended in an argument over an emotional movie we were both passionate about.

The sentiment of learning to adjust and adapt to my wife's nature has been inspiring. I now recognize that her attention span is short and she bounces between topics. Occasionally, she forestalls engagements of sharing and expressing her feelings, which leads to self-imposed stress. The style of her nature has been a challenge. My desires and selfish needs to change her and force my understanding on her in all forms have been kept to a minimum when these situations arise.

We can learn to embrace others' personalities and adapt to changes in their behavior. Show empathy instead of forcing them to change their ways. Remember the values, and respond with love, appreciation, and understanding.

Appreciation and gratitude can help restrain anger and frustration, which is one of the keys to any long-lasting, healthy relationship.

SEARCHING FOR SOULMATES

"We are the creators of our soulmate."

I went to my first concert as an adult with my wife. I'm not the concert type, I kept repeating to myself. This time was different, breaking old ways to try new things. The inability to socialize was ingrained in my personality, permitting avoidance of large crowds.

My wife came across an ad with an artist she knew I liked, Lana Del Rey. I was shocked! To think she was coming to the small city of Brandon, Mississippi! My wife suggested we go.

"Let's do it!" I immediately answered.

Tickets were sold out within days, but I was lucky to find two through a third-party website. Without worry, I waited a month for the tickets to arrive electronically.

As the day approached, the excitement eclipsed the fear of large crowds. Though the artist was an hour late to her set, the date night was perfect. My wife and I enjoyed our time together, while the children were at home, asleep with their grandmother. Moments like this feed our thankfulness for each other and add vigor and longevity, contributing to the security of our marriage.

After being together for seventeen years and married for twelve, it has become natural for me to get gas for my wife and open doors. She dislikes getting gas herself, and I have been doing it for so long that it seems part of our routine. And I have come to appreciate her little quirks.

One of the most remarkable accomplishments in life is to live and share it with someone we love. Unfortunately, this idea has been long forgotten by many.

We are destined to find our soulmate, though we must first find ourselves. I used to agree with the idea that there is one perfect person out there for each of us, but now, with confidence, I know that anyone can be for us. Anyone can be my soulmate, and I could be theirs.

We become one's soulmate by growing beyond our limitations and sharing a deep connection that can reside within anyone. Why are the people in our past relationships able to find someone they can connect with and share their lives with? I could have been that person.

Most people in our past have moved on. Some have found new partners. Some may have been referred to as "crazy," but they found someone who accepted and appreciated their personality. It is possible we could have been the one for each other. Instead of waiting for others to change and adapt to our growth, we can work on ourselves and try to grow alongside those we love and care for.

Why is it always the other person who is mostly at fault in our relationships? We often believe the other person needs to change or has changed for the worse, but not us. Why is it difficult for us to change and adapt to them? It seems much easier to demand change from others than to reflect and admit our faults. To self-improve and self-progress, we must admit our flaws and vices. Only then can we construct successful relationships. When we control ourselves entirely, we can discover our soulmates—it is within us.

Emotions and feelings come and go, especially at the beginning of relationships. Things that would typically bother and annoy us are suppressed by happy feelings. Everything is perfect, but minor things become significant red flags when we overlook them.

When times of despair sink in, our commitment will be tested. You always hear, "Find that spark again." That spark and fire is appreciation and gratitude. Appreciation and respect for each other go a long way. Once the joyful feelings and euphoric sensations are gone and emptied, we allow the unsatisfied feelings to set in. Frequent disagreements begin to shape the relationship. Realize that arguments are not always a bad thing. They can be beneficial in understanding one another.

As we do in life, relationships go through phases. The lifespan of relationships depends on recognizing the phases. When the "honeymoon" phase fizzles out, we may experience years of discontent, disconnect, unappreciation, and falling out of love. Fight for each other during those times and find the gratitude and appreciation that you once had. Know that with time, this too shall pass.

CHAPTER ELEVEN

OUR FAMILY

APPRECIATION IS A FORM OF LOVE

"Compromise the feeling of wanting to be right."

WHILE GRATITUDE IS A form of appreciation, both are essential to a relationship and to driving love. All marriages go through phases. We must identify our weaknesses and face them with commitment and discipline. When moments of appreciation and gratitude disappear, understand that things will get better with time. Be diligent and fight the emptiness, as you still care and have ultimate love for one another.

At times, you hear, "I want to be appreciated." Those are times when happy feelings have faded, and we live in discontent. Find ways to show your partner that you appreciate his or her existence. Speaking and performing actions frequently will add fortitude and help regain an appreciation for one another. Once you lose appreciation for each other, you start to feel resentment. Things that were not an issue before now become one. Irritation begins to develop—you start comparing how much you have done for each other—resulting in dissatisfaction.

When you have meaningless debates and arguments to prove one's fault, resentment sets in. When the happy, positive thoughts run low, your mind, body, and heart are filled with negativity and frustration. Your energy focuses only on the unfavorable things. Replace selfish thoughts with thoughts of gratitude and appreciation.

If you don't replace selfish thoughts, you will become negative as time goes by. There will be nothing there to combat the negativity. You will begin to seek and confide in others, friends and family who typically would agree with you. Instead of agreeing with their opinions, we can simply listen and support without expressing our opinions and views. They seek and want validation for being right in their arguments. Agreeing with them only solidifies their beliefs. When they return to their partner, the confidence of righteousness enables them to be more disconnected from their partner when future issues arise.

We feel hopeless and as though we are just going through the motions, saying to ourselves, I'm just here. We become unhappy and unfulfilled and live in a pattern, making everyday life dull and meaningless.

Unpleasant thoughts run unchecked through our helpless minds. We are easily affected by outside influences when we have been weakened by pain, sadness, and hurt. Once the happy feelings have disappeared, we tend to search for happiness in others, as that route is more accessible than recapturing the joy and appreciation from our current partner. While we do not have existing, unpleasant feelings toward new relationships, it is effortless to receive the validated feeling and love that we seek, as this usually results in cheating.

Everyone wants to be right; no one wants to be wrong. Our nature tends to channel the focus to who's right and wrong. It isolates us and we seek validation to prove whose words are correct. Not every decision has to be right or wrong. Options and possibilities exist.

The more we try to impose and force understanding, the more we believe in our perception of reality, and the more right we think we are. We run the risk of creating a divide between us and others. Resentment can build when we force ourselves to adapt to others without compassion. We become inconsistent when we consistently try to be right.

Eliminate words like "right" and "wrong." Reply to disagreements with "yes, and..." followed by an explanation. It allows a lighter, more sensitive, and less aggressive approach to counter differences. Apologies will ascend the relationship to its peak and develop character.

Separate from the emphasis on being right. Understand there are other approaches. We can share an understanding and different perspectives without the prefixes of what is right and wrong. We can respond to aggression and hateful words with kindness and forgiveness.

It is our nature to defend our feelings, so we redirect and cast blame onto others. The sentiments of compromise are neglected. When seeking change in others is unsuccessful, we are tested to adapt and change ourselves when control is not within our grasp. Control what is in your power and not of any outside force. You cannot control what others think, say, or do, but you can control how you respond.

Moments of frustration and anger can occur. When tensions run high, we can find ways to replace our anger and frustration with compassion and forgiveness, which helps to contain negative emotions and adapt to unwanted situations.

There may be times, under certain circumstances, when we cannot remove and distance ourselves from a negative situation completely. We can either allow compassion and forgiveness to combat the emotions of anger and resentment or continue to live in misery with our hate. Compassion and forgiveness are the antidote for anger and hate. The pain and suffering others may cause us can be treated with love and kindness. Our forgiveness may allow some words of compassion to touch them.

Senseless, hateful words come from an unhappy place. Do not allow words of hate to penetrate and affect your emotions. Safeguard your peace and happiness. Our minds become more transparent when we share advice, opinions, and views because our emotions are contained, and our feelings are not jeopardized. We can acclimate to respond with compassion and acts of kindness to preserve our sanity. Be disciplined and capture your emotions when the situation arises. Go beyond the bounds of understanding.

You are competent in controlling yourself with unlimited possibilities. Exceed your imaginary lines and boundaries. Some may have lines and boundaries they will not cross or are incapable of crossing, and some can surpass their feelings and thoughts.

Right and wrong should not be associated with whether we halt at the boundary or go farther. There is no right or wrong way to take different routes and paths to reach your inner peace. All these paths lead to the same place. When acknowledging the possibilities—you are capable of such thoughts and acts—you can come to peace with yourself.

STAYING TOGETHER FOR THE CHILDREN

"Dialogue daily. Date regularly. Retreat yearly."

Recently, I attended a five-week men's Bible study titled Better Man, led by Pastor Kyle Reno, at my children's school. The study focused on loving our women. The attendance was large. After the first session and group conversations, I realized that no matter what stage you are in your marriage or relationship, there is always room for growth.

You should never stop improving yourself, as there is no limit to how much you can improve. I adopted a quote from Pastor Kyle that has since become my motto: "Dialogue daily. Date regularly. Retreat yearly." This quote has been a reminder to continue to date my wife and keep improving the relationship.

Before the birth of my first child, an elderly couple who'd been married for fifty years gave me a wise piece of advice: "Husband and wife come first, then the children." Initially, it sounded selfish, but as it began to marinate, with further analysis and digging deeper, I grasped its true meaning. Since then, I have lived by this statement.

Societal influence has changed the values of relationships. It is becoming more challenging to achieve longevity. Longer marriages are becoming rare because sacrifice and commitment have changed their course.

Maintaining a nuclear family and happiness within the home starts from the top: husband and wife, the parents. The responsibility falls on the parents, as working equally hard on the marriage is essential. Parents should make time for each other to strengthen their relationship, as it can impact the children's lives if we selfishly cannot unite as parents. Not only will this have a negative effect on the child, but the child is more likely to repeat the same behavior.

Staying together for the children's sake can also prolong and fortify the relationship, even after the children have grown and moved out. This way, parents can avoid feeling empty and without purpose or struggling to reignite the spark that once brought the family together. However, it is not always beneficial for the children. We garner the ability to sacrifice our individual needs and desires and place our children before us. Children should not bear the brunt of their parents' thoughtless and self-centered decisions.

LEAD BY EXAMPLE

"I no longer want to be a hypocrite. My actions and behaviors will be consistent with my words."

"Dad, can I come to Bible study with you?" Max asked me when he heard I was attending another men's Bible study.

I said, "Of course you can, but it's very early in the morning. I wake up at five. I'm going to wake you up once. If you don't wake up, I'm leaving you, sir."

Motivated, Max woke up early without struggle, and we were out the door by five-forty in the morning.

Although he sometimes slept at the Bible study, having this father-son bonding time outside of sports was a price-less joy beyond words. This experience helped show him my relationship and devotion to God and helped shape me into who I am today.

He and I discussed the positive impact of faith and spirituality on one's life and how it can provide guidance and support during difficult times. I also showed him the various communities available and how impactful they are. We talked about the importance of surrounding ourselves with good influences and how this can help us become better individuals. I showed him the people I surround myself with and how they have helped me grow and develop.

As a parent, I am responsible for providing my children with a positive environment and guiding them toward the right path. As adults, we can mindfully surround ourselves with good influences, just as we want our children to be surrounded by them. We teach our children to surround themselves with positive influences, yet sometimes we forget and fail to do the same as adults.

Studies have shown that the most influential people in children's lives are not their parents but rather the parents of their friends and their teachers, coaches, and communities. The environment where they grow up, rather than their parents, is a significant determinant of their future wealth and success.

Apprehending this, I have made a conscious effort to focus on my children's surroundings, which has positively impacted their lives. Children often imitate their parents—boys mimic their fathers, while girls tend to emulate their mothers. They should have a balance of one parent's nurturing and caring support and the other parent's discipline and toughness.

Without the presence of my stepfather, Franko, who took me in at a young age, I may not have grown into the man I am today. I lived without structure and discipline, running the streets with the "wrong crowd," and I was also a bad influence on others.

In many ways, I later modeled myself on Franko. Hard worker, stern, disciplined, humble, health conscious, clean; I did not possess these traits before he entered my life. The importance of a man with moral family values in a home cannot be taken lightly; it may have a significant imprint on a child's life.

Rediscovering my profound role in my boys' lives, I have devoted myself to setting a good example and being a positive role model for them, my friends' children, and others children—not only with words but through my actions and behavior. I know they will pick up after me in everything I do. Though it may be challenging to become their role model, I know it is achievable. We have to discipline ourselves when disciplining our children.

Generally, we teach children to do the right thing, make good choices, and practice self-discipline. I am guilty of using the phrase, "Do as I say, not as I do." How hypocritical of me to tell the children not to copy and mimic what I do—this is precisely what they do at that age. They absorb knowledge and behaviors and form characteristics of those they look up to and admire, based on the examples they see around them.

However, as adults, we often struggle to discipline ourselves and make wise decisions, especially when it comes to addictive behaviors. Sometimes, we even lose control of our emotions and yell at our kids, telling them to stop crying or behave while we cannot control our temper. This may confuse the children as they grow up and face conflicts in adulthood.

I used to get angry, frustrated, and yell when disciplining my children. I used to deal with and release stress through anger. However, I've recognized the importance of modeling self-control and emotional regulation for my children. Now, I consciously choose to speak to them calmly and assertively to show them that we can effectively control our emotions. I strive to lead by example in handling challenging situations.

I realized that forgiving and guiding them through their poor decisions is essential, rather than expressing anger. Allow them to experience life. By teaching them how to respond positively to their experiences and mistakes, I hope to instill moral values and lessons that will help them build character.

The teachings of discipline and values remain the same in our home, though different teaching methods may suit certain personalities better. Therefore, I cannot teach my two sons the same way.

I used to aspire to provide them with everything, shelter them from life's hardships, and give them the world. But my perspective has evolved, and I know the importance of them earning their way. I want them to earn it and experience the process. I must allow them to learn from their mistakes, not prevent them from making them.

No matter how much wisdom, knowledge, and guidance I impart, I recognize that sometimes life will teach them in ways I cannot. Whatever the outcome, the hurt I may bear, I must let them experience life.

The objective is to teach kids to grow without regrets and to embrace their mistakes. One day, I want to convey to my sons that I have reached a point where I no longer make mistakes. Still, I confidently stand by my decisions and gracefully accept the outcomes, understanding that each outcome contributes to my journey.

I want to help my sons quell their fears and conquer themselves—maximize their chances of success and never give up on life. They can achieve anything with the right motivation and faith.

CHAPTER TWELVE

CONDITIONING THE MIND

FINDING THE BALANCE

*"Contradictions serve as a reminder
that balance exists."*

USUALLY, WHEN SOMEONE HAS been away from social media for an extended period, the assumption that something traumatic has happened in their life comes to mind.

It has been months since I have visited any social media platforms, and they have become meaningless and dull. Short-term self-gratification was the source of seeking fatuous interactions on social media. I no longer have the desire to search for feelings of approval to help cope with stress and depression.

Further contributing to a broken society, possessions have become glorified with the endless quest for false pleasures. I had fallen victim to material values, enslaved by the influence of what I thought would gain respect and approval from society. I noticed a change in myself—I became increasingly impulsive about material possessions. I had lost sight of what truly matters.

Social conditioning has influenced fallacious judgments and views. Our society has succeeded in controlling the consumption of short-term happiness through social media. When boredom presents itself, we are engrossed in entertaining ourselves, unknowingly allowing character-istics of addiction to form. This begins to affect our lives negatively, and we replace the idea of self-improvement with false desires.

The media bombards us with news that often triggers outrage and destructive emotions, leading to chaos, division, and isolation. Its primary purpose is stimulating our minds with negativity and objectively provoking an emotional response. We have become numb to the news of violence, shootings, and killings—uninterested in the good news.

We often seek immediate solutions to long-term prob-lems, but there are none. However, quick fixes usually lead to new issues that are more complex and difficult to address. Therefore, adopting a more proactive and comprehensive approach to problem-solving is crucial.

One way to address these issues is to start at home by instilling values and discipline in ourselves and our families. We can do this by practicing empathy, honesty, compas-sion, and respect daily. As we model these values, we help create a culture of integrity and mutual support in our communities.

Schools play a significant role in shaping our future. By providing students with a well-rounded education that includes academic knowledge and social and emotional learning, we can help them develop the skills and values necessary to become responsible and productive members of society. This education includes teaching critical thinking, effective communication, and collaboration. Addressing long-term problems requires a holistic approach that instills good values and morals at home and provides a comprehensive school education. Implementing Christian values and morals mindfully with human rights may create a more compassionate and just society where everyone can thrive.

While family and skill-set values are highly regarded in other countries, the United States has misled our youth with disinformation and misguided values. The ongoing global issues and evolving social standards have outweighed the previously highly esteemed idea of starting a family. As a result, families are becoming smaller, and communities are shrinking. This has led to increased seclusion among individuals and even families.

The state of the environment and limited resources in certain areas have conditioned and forced us to focus solely on fending for ourselves. This is the result of populating without a family system. Strong family values and communities are the tools that can unite us to build a prosperous economy.

Though human rights should be highly valued, they have taken a different turn and, in some cases, weakened the minds of youth. There is a concern that their interpretation and implementation have had unintended consequences, particularly in relation to the impact on the mental resilience of our youth. We must recognize and remember the value of accountability and discipline in shaping a responsible and respectful society.

My new outlook and beliefs have drastically changed my views on abortion, and I am now on the side of life. This sensitive topic and issue continues to divide our country. The most selfless responsibility is creating life. The act of making a life should be a responsibility that is highly regarded and valued.

Human rights are used to excuse us from our irresponsible mistakes. Reproductive rights should not overshadow irresponsibility and accountability. Every choice that we make affects that life at the beginning of conception. How we value life is how we value our choices. Learn and embrace your mistakes; do not try to erase or eliminate them. The circumstances of our conception do not define our value.

Distractions from various forms of entertainment have slowly distorted our way of life. We indulge in immediate, pointless entertainment to help us forget our struggles and problems. Though it helps us deal with and cope with stress, pain, suffering, and depression, it blindly masks and isolates our ability to find ways to help ourselves. Once the endorphins have faded, depression circles back tenfold.

Reinvent yourself, rewire your brain, and break free from the constraints of a flawed society.

I think an initial, seeded thought or idea becomes a fact with repetition. We equivocally believe just to fit in and be part of a group. We often adopt these ideas and behaviors without any critical thinking or analysis of their validity. To avoid this, we can train and recondition our minds to differentiate subconsciously and become more aware of the ideas we accept as facts. Balance the accessibility of content and information while maintaining its quality and accuracy.

We must consciously choose the ideas we accept as facts rather than mindlessly following the crowd, becoming normalized to the ideas, and unknowingly adopting the behaviors. By doing so, we can avoid being inadvertently conditioned to believe and behave in ways that do not align with our true values and beliefs. Our minds are overtly complex yet we can be simple-minded creatures and easily influenced.

SPIRITUAL WARFARE

"A peaceful world starts with inner peace."

Why are we susceptible to gossip and drama? Do we unconsciously seek and are drawn to the troubles in others' lives to help us forget our struggles? Or is it a way to remind ourselves we are not the only ones with problems?

Our current state of mind and well-being largely influence how we inherit information. Feeling happy and positive, we are more receptive to criticism and teachings. However, when we are feeling down, angry, depressed, or stressed, we tend to be unreceptive and respond with negativity. This is due to our unconscious defensive mechanism, which protects us from anxious thoughts and feelings. Nevertheless, we can change our ways and become more receptive to living a happier and more productive life. Realize, hidden deep within us, that we all desire to improve and become better versions of ourselves.

Societal issues, government, politics—these subjects have occupied my life and distracted me from God. I was responding to life without God, allowing myself to indulge in meaningless pursuits. My changing perspectives on life have greatly impacted my life with God.

Being unable to fully isolate from the media regarding the strife and war in Israel, all I can do is pray and teach my sons to do the same. We pray for everyone in Israel, both the good and bad. We need to prepare and educate the younger generations on responding to wars and tragedies without being negatively affected.

We seem uninterested in the good news. However, we can contribute by continuing to improve ourselves, learn, and pass down knowledge to younger generations so they may one day acquire the wisdom to prevent wars and achieve peace.

Humanistic religious wars have had lingering effects on our society and are still present today in the form of individual spiritual warfare. These conflicts arise from the trauma, loss, and disillusionment people experienced during those times. As a result, many individuals struggle to find meaning and purpose, feeling disconnected from their communities and themselves.

Acknowledging the past and working toward healing these wounds can help individuals find a sense of belonging and meaning in their lives. Promoting empathy, compassion, and understanding can create a more cohesive society where individuals feel valued and supported. Although healing takes time, we can overcome the harmful effects of past wars with patience and persistence.

I no longer prioritize race, country, religion, or government. The path has brought me to the realization that none of those matters. I am on the side of humanity. Replace our differences with faith, love, empathy, compassion, and forgiveness. Negativity has influenced our society to focus on our differences, enhancing self-exaltation.

Although we may say "race does not matter" and "I see no color," our behaviors appear to be influenced by pride. The pridefulness of our country and ethnicity tends to disregard others; we, in turn, separate ourselves, and race becomes the focal point for many of our issues. Pride and judgment are the root of our problems, hidden beneath our physical and cultural differences. We often create divisions between ourselves and our neighbors due to variations in our beliefs and perspectives.

I acknowledge that every system is flawed due to human nature's inherent flaws. Therefore, I will stay devoted to self-improvement. This is my contribution to society, the world, and humanity.

Is it possible to lead without power, without consuming wealth (because gaining power and wealth will eventually lead to corruption)?

Human nature's flaws corrupt every system, but change is possible. We can lead by example and inspire others to do the same. Change starts with us. Until then, we are contributing only to society's demise. We cannot control external events but focus on what we can control. By focusing on what we can maintain and constantly improving ourselves, we can create a brighter future for ourselves and those around us. Bettering ourselves is critical to managing our lives. As we improve individually, we can one day live peacefully and cohesively in any system.

The path to destruction has clearly presented itself. We live in the most comfortable, convenient time in human history, yet we are fearful and suffering. Envy and comparison have stripped us of happiness and swayed us from appreciating life.

Acknowledge that these distractions persuade us away from a relationship with God. We are fighting a battle for our minds. Wars will always exist while there is inner warfare.

We can unite only when we step back and progress to self-improve, self-reflect, and self-educate. One day, humanity will break through our physical and mental differences. Rediscover, improve, and forgive. Then we may forgive others and live among one another with righteousness and love.

We all desire the same thing: to be a good person, peace, love, and free will to choose without negative judgments. Although we have different ways and approaches, we are met with the evilness of the world. As fallible human beings, there will be a time when we will all agree and come to a middle ground with world issues, politics, and human rights, as we are all rooted with the same desire for peace.

FORCEFUL BEHAVIOR

"How can I help others understand my views and perspectives if I cannot effectively communicate my new positive outlook on life with loved ones and friends?"

Politics has become a form of entertainment. Obsessed with politics and keeping up with current events, I had lost sight of why it became an interest of mine in the first place. I concerned myself only with government and politics, and I had an interest only once I had a family and realized the impact of politics on our lives. Thinking of my family and my new self, I became determined to help change our country, government, and environment. But all I contributed was divisive opinions and views, which helped separate our country even more.

"Andy, it's a big club, and we're not in it," my brother-in-law Jonathan reminded me. A club of wealthy, powerful elites beyond my grasp. Other than formulating negative opinions and views, I have little control and minimal impact.

Being forceful with my politics and too assertive with my opinions caused me to overlook the importance of listening and understanding other people's perspectives. All it did was reinforce my existing opinions, as I focused solely on expressing my viewpoints. Even with a less aggressive approach, I strenuously imposed my political views on others to make them care and take interest. But my methods needed to be corrected. I thought I was adept in the subject matter and wanted to be correct, on the right side, as we all do. No one wants to be wrong in this fight.

For now, while I further seek to educate and improve myself, the day may come when I can discover different methods and approaches to addressing politics, world issues, and my beliefs. Therefore, I have elected to distance myself from the negative effects of politics and the news.

Compassion and empathy have changed my political views while I distance myself. I am on the right and left, with no attachment to any party. I aspire to conduct future conversations driven by love and positivity to share different views with others—lead with empathy everywhere I go, with every conversation I have. I can fully immerse myself in topics and issues with compassionate opinions in debates. However, I am still searching for a balance that will enable me to express my thoughts and achieve the wisdom to receive information without bias. Some of us are flawed to the point that seeing the goodness in others is difficult.

The more we surround ourselves with like-minded individuals, the more we isolate ourselves from diverse perspectives. This leads to a stronger attachment to our beliefs and opinions. We can approach those with different views, opinions, and attitudes with kindness and an open heart. Yet, when removing ourselves is an option, we can distance ourselves from unfavorable circumstances beyond our control. Interactions and conversations with negative energy will lead only to aggression and hate, which, unfortunately, are common in our society.

With the fast growth of technology and being in the service industry, it is sometimes hard to seclude myself. However, I avoid the false, negative energy stemming from the news and online interactions as best as I can. The negative effects of social media and human interactions have taught me that silence is often the language of the wise. Past energy had been fueled by negativity, aggression, and self-absorption. Consequently, with the vast consumption of social media, our country was led down the path of destruction.

You have one body, mind, soul, and life in this world. What are you if you cannot control yourself, your mind, thoughts, emotions, feelings, mouth, and actions?

Be in control of your mind and destiny and remind yourself that you are every morning. Each day, anger, frustration, and stress will present themselves less. Controlling your thoughts is the first step in self-discipline. Without control, you cannot govern your actions. Instinctively, aggressive words trigger and drive straight to our emotions, while calm words engage our minds.

While I seek a life of faith, I have yet to balance my new beliefs and the need to proceed with mindfulness. This has led me to delve into why Jesus proceeded to wash his twelve disciples' feet. I realized that it was necessary to lead them with an understanding. My past self would never have been comfortable allowing the act to happen—I would force myself through it. I am not worthy, I would think. I would be disrespecting Him. My uncomfortableness would not allow me to receive the meaning.

In a way, the display of His sacrifice, humility, and forgiveness of their sins through spiritual cleansing also showed Him sacrificing their sense of discomfort to achieve an understanding contrary to theirs. He had faith that the discernment would come. The act would not yield discomfort or shame, for I now see the underlying purpose.

The limits we place on the standard within our understanding are the only things that limit our minds.

DISCOVERING CALMNESS IN MUSIC

"Music is a tool that can be used for good and evil."

My taste in music has profoundly changed in response to the powerful transformation in my spirit, elevating my experience. I had once preferred trance and techno, as they exude youthful energy. Additionally, my younger self related to the anger and aggression often found in hip-hop. As years passed, my taste in music broadened to other genres when new life experiences were encountered. I found myself in recurrent phases of alternative rock and love songs when relationships blossomed and shriveled.

My choice of music has drastically changed from slow and depressing to happy, upbeat, up-tempo music with positive and kind words. Looking back, when I was in a negative state of mind, slow, depressing rhythms and hateful words were the choice of music when I was at the gym four to five times a week.

Full of life, pure and innocent, with abundant, joyful energy, Max introduced me to his playlist. As I listened to and liked it, I no longer enjoyed the slow, depressing, negative music that once invoked my interest while working out.

Every morning since discovering my path, the boys and I sing, dance, and act silly on our way to school without embarrassment or fear of others watching us. I began to notice that I have been living with joy, love, and positivity, and for that, I thank my son Max.

Christian music—a genre I was apathetic toward—has become a warmth of sunshine and delight. My new love for Christian music has increased every time it is played during church. It adds potency to the journey. I realize that music does not affect our mood, our current state of mind. Rather, our mood and the stage in our lives, whether positive or negative, influence our interest in music.

We all go through stages in life where we experience love, creativity, joy, and hope. There are also times when we are drenched with absolute sadness, depression, anger, heartache, and pain.

As we deal with a breakup, we enjoy music about love, pain, relationships, and sorrow. These types of music enhance our existing emotions and intensify our feelings even more; they prolong our feelings. Allow time to heal the feelings and, instead, seek joyful music.

My playlist for the last few weeks has consisted of songs from the Lana Del Rey concert. They are slow and depressing. Waking up the family for school and working with the music, I noticed slight changes in my writing and the aura within the home. Max's attitude changed instantly. He became more defiant with sudden mood swings. My wife and I engaged in a few mild debates, none of which were warranted.

I have realized that certain words, combined with musical rhythms, can influence and dictate our behaviors and emotions. Upon discovering this, I hastily reverted to the soothing, rhythmic melodies, as they provided calm, mental stimulation. The intuition yielded instant positive changes in my son's attitude and behavior and the overall mood within the house. Peace began to reappear throughout the home.

Despite the extensive basic concept of enjoying music throughout our lives and society, mainstream awareness of music therapy has been suppressed. Research and evidence demonstrate the effects of frequencies on health, aligning with ancient practices.

Studies have shown that most illnesses are associated with stress. As a result, various treatments in sound therapy can help alleviate stress, promote relaxation, and effectively treat and prevent illnesses. Additionally, sound therapy has been known to reduce headaches and lower blood pressure. Certain frequencies and vibrations can trigger the release of endorphins, while specific frequencies have the ability to alter our DNA and impact biological systems, resulting in long-lasting effects.

Therefore, be conscious of the ethical use of sound. Sound can heal and provide comfort but can also hurt and distract. Music is a form of conditioning; it can be controlled positively or negatively.

More knowledge of the significant impact of sound frequencies on our physical and psychological state should be widespread. Music can cure illnesses and provide internal happiness—or lead to self-destruction.

CHAPTER THIRTEEN

BATTLING INNER DEMONS

IDENTIFYING NEGATIVE ENERGY

"Why do I frequently have negative and awful thoughts?"

PACKING MICAH'S SCHOOL LUNCH, I realized the impact of society and the environment on our thought process. I could not help but wonder if it was unusual that he liked to drink only water. Should I introduce him to sugary drinks? Am I helping to suppress my child from a fun, carefree childhood?

These thoughts immediately made me question myself and how our society can influence us to oppose a child enjoying water. However, I understand the influence of greed and profit. Why do I give my children access to the things I am trying to quit and eliminate from my life as an adult? Why do I avoid eating at fast-food restaurants and still feed it to my children? Seeing how these societal norms can heavily influence our thinking is concerning. Our evaluations can enable us to identify these influences and determine whether to break away from them.

I have analyzed the changes and why positive thoughts have overtaken unpleasant ones. I train to respond positively to daily situations, which helps suppress negative thoughts. We must identify the thoughts that are not influenced by the Holy Spirit and adjust our minds to think and generate positive thoughts constantly. We can create and manifest more positive than negative ones.

Replace negative energy and ideas with positive and loving thoughts. Getting rid of every negative and dark thought is crucial, as it can grow and lead to bad judgments and decisions. Once we reanimate our minds, we will begin to feel calmer and be able to counter any adverse situation with control and a more positive outlook. Be in control of the negativity.

LIVING WITH EMPATHY

"The more negative energy we possess, the more negative thoughts we generate."

Four days before Halloween, my wife called, distressed while heading home from work. A vehicle had approached Max.

"I have candy in the truck. Do you want to come inside?" a strange man asked Max. Terrified, Max turned and rushed inside the house to tell his mother.

Distraught and pacing through the kitchen, my wife tried to relay the details as I walked into the house. Calm and clear, I proceeded to call the police. Afterward, I shared the information and experience online to inform neighbors and the community. My old self and many fathers alike would have responded aggressively and with fury. To protect my children, I would have turned to a darker side.

Lighter thoughts have resonated within—positive thoughts of how I would handle the situation if I were in contact with the strange man. A more aggressive and physical approach may only satisfy our anger and emotions, in addition to further displacing one's reality. Aggression and anger may feed a person's warped reality, but I believe a less aggressive approach may induce the possibility of change.

I have always had negative thoughts about how I would deal with and respond to a traumatic event, such as if I had an illness. How would I react or proceed with my life if my wife or mother were diagnosed with cancer or a fatal disease? I would conjure thoughts of different tragic situations, responding with sadness and hopelessness, dwelling in sorrow, and selfishly seeking sympathy and attention from others.

Now, looking back at those dark thoughts, a brighter, more uplifting outlook has been inserted in my mind. Rather than craving attention and sympathy from others, think positively, I tell myself. *It will be all right. I deserve a better life and better thoughts.*

By embracing positive energy, I have allowed it to replace the negative feelings of sadness, pain, anger, sorrow, loneliness, and all other unpleasant emotions. I can honestly say that in the face of unfortunate future events, I will relish the beautiful moments. Within those moments, *I know I will be fine. I will be all right. I will focus on the children.* My wife and I have blessed each other with two beautiful boys. Faith and hopefulness will fuel my confidence. Strength will preserve this philosophy for the remainder of my life.

Empathy has engulfed my new mind; every situation has been treated with this outlook. I now categorize worry and stress as negative energy. My mind became more apparent, allowing me to distinguish between opposing forces and resist the thoughts of evil hidden behind the negativity. Identifying thoughts made it easier to get rid of the energy. When consumed with stress and worry, we lose control of our emotions and focus on things that we cannot change. This ultimately dictates and consumes how we respond to situations and events. Negative thoughts will only result in negative judgments, decisions, and outcomes.

THE ENEMY

"Discover the flaws in your happiness."

Years ago, a client lost her young son. With the recent passing, she came and had services done at the salon, and I judged her. I thought, Why is she here? Why is she not home grieving? Why does she selfishly need a luxury fix? I was in a different state of mind—hateful and self-indulgent.

Looking back, I wish I had sent positive energy to her. Compassion had abandoned me. The selfish feelings had overtaken my sense of empathy. The negative response resulted from how I thought I would feel and behave after a personal tragedy. That negative energy was dominant and may have reached and added to her pain.

As we brace ourselves for these painful and tragic events, remember that we have the power to choose how we let them affect us. I choose to let them influence me in a positive light. I will allow my experience and feelings to positively impact those around me by sharing love and strength with my loved ones rather than burdening them with my grief.

We target only the unfortunate things that have happened or why they happened. Why am I experiencing this? I should have done this. I should have done that. This creates more negativity. Why indulge in negative energy, stress, and misery for past events or future ones that may not happen? Focus on the present and your mind will steer clear of bad judgments.

When we are weak and unable to control our emotions and negative thoughts, we tend to respond to daily situations with aggression, anger, and hate. By occupying ourselves with love and positivity, we can better control how we react to negative situations, which will spawn positive solutions.

At times, I lose control of myself and wonder who is in control of my body if not me. I want to train my mind and gain complete control over it, not allowing the flesh to control me. I aim to achieve absolute control of my physical body, inside and out, and never lose control again.

Let your mind regain control of your body, not surrender to emotions and feelings. We can fill ourselves with love, opening our hearts and allowing positive energy to take over. The feelings become controllable. This will give us the ability and alertness to make better judgments and choices. We bring adverse outcomes by responding with negative energy, aggression, hate, and anger. The work of the evil spirit consumes us. Worry consumes us, making us lifeless and unmotivated, and we focus only on our failures, seeking instant results and handouts.

We can let our devastations defeat us and bring us to self-destruction or let them motivate us to overcome failures and progress. Our mental habits can become lazy as we seek instant gratification and external approval to cope with negativity. We seek various social media platforms, such as shows, news, and movies, for meaningless, temporary enjoyment. Entertaining ourselves becomes a gateway to our troubles. As a result, bad habits begin to form.

Though I am further into having received the light, the dark thoughts have slowly found their way back, reappearing in small doses. Sometimes I get random thoughts about old habits and addictions. *Who and what is generating these thoughts? Where do these thoughts originate? Are they coming from an unconscious place?* While I ask these questions and assess the recent stretches of positive thoughts, the dark thoughts reappear. Even thinking of harmless, little white lies wakes and feeds my demons; I feel as though they eat away at my soul. Although contradicting thoughts have surfaced, I have not deviated from the path. But I have now come to understand that these thoughts are not indeed mine.

I recognize that the enemy influences them. But they have become minuscule and carry no weight. Recognizing the slight change, I turned to meditation and affirmations of my newfound faith. While in the state of meditation, my emptied mind slowly progressed into graceful thoughts—and meditations gradually became prayers. Having experienced the capability of reproducing blissful thoughts, I was able to break free from the shackles of negativity. I do not stress and worry; I pray.

Finding balance is the key to peace, the answer to living well. There is a balance between everything in life, including knowledge. Acquiring too much knowledge without balance and control can be just as harmful as having little knowledge. Sometimes, we need help to balance the information we receive. As the info expands, our perception of reality can be susceptible to negative influences. Without balance, vast knowledge can attract the enemy.

I often developed opinions and views without delving deeper into the subject and seeking more knowledge and information. I failed to become mindful and find a balance. The information I acquired led to isolating my opinions and beliefs from those of others. Our sinful nature overrides our love, forgiveness, and compassion, which can further drive us to group, categorize, and separate ourselves. Therefore, it is essential to be more open to knowledge from all types and sources and approach it sensibly. Although we are all different, we are similar in many ways. We all experience the same emotions and feelings but express them differently, live our lives in distinct ways, and share unique stories.

I fear that too much money, wisdom, and knowledge may lead me away from God. I favor ample knowledge and insight to secure fellowship with Him. Having too much or too little of something can have negative consequences. Excess or deficiency of anything can lead to our downfall. It is crucial to maintain a balance in all aspects of our lives to avoid potential harm. We should consume life in moderation.

Things that were once valued and considered necessary are no longer essential. I have squandered my life and money on sinful pursuits. True happiness became more challenging and complex to touch, while false pleasure abundantly appeared. Pursuing happiness was a mistake. I needed to allow it to happen and embrace it when it came and went. Pursuing happiness is flawed, as it is not always synonymous with goodness. Despite finding joy in sinful behavior, blissfulness can exist in every aspect of life and create bliss in any situation.

OUR MOST VALUABLE ASSET IS TIME

*"Appreciate the little things and
discover the joy in them."*

Writing has become my way of balancing and containing positive and negative energies. I bring my computer everywhere; I write at work, in parking lots, at the park, on the back porch, and any time of the day I can squeeze some words in. In addition to writing, coaching, working at the nail salon, working out, and Bible study, I picked up an extra job for an online taxi service, referred by my friend and client, Rhonda.

With a second chance to live, I was humbled to drive strangers around town while balancing my busy schedule. Although I drove around in a gas-guzzling SUV like a senior citizen, slow and usually in the right lane, the human interactions were well worth the time. I would sit and converse for thirty minutes upon arriving in front of a rider's house, which may not have been financially beneficial to me. Deep down, maybe the actual reasoning was to spread positivity and a sprinkle of faith here and there.

All my life, I used to think that there was abundant time. The twenty-four-hour day felt too lengthy, but now it seems there always needs to be more. We can either create an excess of time or a shortage of it. Do not waste precious time on meaningless pursuits; use it wisely.

You do not have to be extraordinary or have an exceptional mind to pursue and understand life without sin. Anyone with a progressing mind can have the courage to live an ordinary life well and meaningfully.

It always starts with a thought or an idea and ends with a choice. It could be a fleeting or deep-seated thought, but it all begins with a single idea. The challenging part is to recognize what lies behind that thought. Sometimes, our thoughts are triggered by past experiences, emotions, or external factors that we may not be aware of. Thus, it's essential to understand our thoughts and the reasons behind them. Once we identify the thought, we decide whether to act on it or remove it from our minds. We all have the power of choice. Every thought leads to a choice, and the choices we make determine the path we take in life.

Drink only (warm) water, eat your vegetables and fruit, eat less meat, take your vitamins, don't sleep late, don't smoke, and exercise regularly. These words and lectures from my mother came in one ear and went right out the other. The unwavering stubbornness grew in my thirties. Every day, I wished she would stop talking, as I was an adult. It took forty-two years to realize that all I needed to do was what she had asked. Now, her speeches and lectures are a thing of the past; they have withered away like leaves.

It took me a significant amount of time to realize that my choices and lack of obedience directly affected my mother's sense of peace. I needed to be obedient to my parents; I needed to be obedient to Him. The time I used to waste is now spent with the Lord.

Your decisions have consequences, and you must be prepared to face them. Take a moment to reflect on your thoughts and choices. Strive to win confidence and contentment in every decision you make. By doing so, you can better understand yourself and make informed judgments.

VIEWING NEW LIFE IN THE SPIRIT

*"The more we act against our convictions,
the less control we have over ourselves."*

I sin whenever I struggle with my conviction. I know it is wrong for me, but I still do it, although I cannot judge or tell anyone that they are sinning. It is between them and God if they choose to believe. The Holy Spirit can fill and replace the feelings of doubt.

I equate the thoughts and behaviors of yelling, cursing, anger, negativity, adultery, all of my prior addictions, unhealthy eating, and even consuming energy drinks to the same sinful value as murder. This is my method of removing these undesirable vices from my life.

I am absolutely confident in my ability not to commit murder. My weaknesses have been my inability to identify and abandon the lesser sins. I have learned to view these actions and assign them the same seriousness and degree, whether major or minor transgressions. I have made a deliberate effort to place them alongside my strengths. In turn, the struggle of my negative convictions has diminished, giving way to the strength of faith. The Holy Spirit has filled and replaced the feelings of doubt.

This will be my first joyful New Year's, when I have not reverted to the old, inconsistent self and the unproductive routine. With a heightened sense of confidence, I yield the courage to confront and overcome my sinful nature. Immersed in God's presence, the spiritual shield thickens and grows stronger. The attacks of the evil spirit now seem feeble and meek. Sin, which once loomed as a daunting force, now appears less intimidating in light of the deepened faith.

I have noticed that the less I sin, the less my mind generates negative thoughts. The more I sin, the more I become a victim of poor judgments, irresponsible choices, and bad decisions. I used my human flaws as an excuse to continue sinning. I had to release the negative energy and evil spirits that had been occupying my mind and physique. Living a better life was stifled by the evil spirit. I was spiritually dead and unable to feel and recognize the sins.

Faith brought life to that part of me that had died. Jesus Christ became my champion and I fought back. As powerful as the addictions and vices had become, they vanished as quickly as lightning in His presence.

I no longer choose to sin, and the intensity of my temptations has lessened. My past sins will not define who I am, diminish my worth, or negate what I am.

The battle with the seven deadly sins lightens each day:

Envy – I have forgiven myself and let go of envy and jealousy. I quit envying others for their success and accomplishments because I can achieve my own success. I have rid myself of the negative energy and can genuinely congratulate others on their achievements. I stopped obsessing about what others possess. I am content and happy with what I have physically, mentally, and materially. It was vital for me to continue to pursue the teachings and values of a quality Christian education at Hartfield Academy for my children.

The influence of status and envy on my mind and their role in feeding my inner demons are long gone.

Gluttony – I am eating healthier, drinking healthier, consuming less, and eating only once a day with an abundant amount of water. Although I have minimized eating fast food, I am still challenged to stay disciplined in not feeding it to my children, as that is negative energy. Eating unhealthy and excessively is a form of addiction.

Greed – My greed and desire to be wealthy and financially successful have diminished. The hunger to win the lottery has dissolved, as it is also negative energy and will only cause more problems. The impulse to give my wife material things was the fuel behind my greed for falsely showcasing wealth. Now wealth and power over others have become meaningless.

Lust – I no longer lust with my eyes and mind while these dark thoughts appear daily. As I encounter beauty at the gym, school, market, work, media, and internet, my immediate drive-by thoughts of lust are now met with love, positivity, and forgiveness. I forgive myself for the dark thoughts as I move on to positive ones. My urges for pornography have been abandoned. The desire for lustful fantasies died with the old Andy. Only my wife has my eye's full attention and interest. We permit our thoughts to be consumed by appetites for lust. Each fleeting idea nourishes our psyche's darker aspects and contributes to our soul's corruption.

Pride – The ultimate prize has always been my pride and shame. Giving up my shame feels like giving up a part of myself that I held dearly and protected. It is a sacrifice I was unwilling to make for a long time, because it meant losing a part of my identity. Pride blinded me to be incapable of forgiveness. I always sought attention with lies of self-accomplishment. I prided myself as a great person, a person of knowledge, and one worth liking. Pride had prevented me from improving and yearning for knowledge. It falsely influenced me to think I was perfect and did not need to change. I realize the power of pride and its impact on my thinking. My mindset and attitude significantly improved when I rid myself of pride.

Sloth – I had feared and avoided learning new things, such as expanding my vocabulary, writing, socializing, and coaching. I was slothful with every decision I made. I now occupy every second, every moment of the day, with productivity. I even dedicated some time to helping at WOL Church, which I never imagined I would do or thought I was worthy of doing. I do not waste my valuable time. I sleep less. But, of course, rest is necessary and encouraged.

Wrath – My inner rage was predicated on the need to be right, which led to frustration, bitterness, and resentment.

Viewing others without judgment has replaced that rage. The ability to forgive myself and others has given me the strength to control my emotions, exchanging anger for calmness. I am filled with positive energy and the confidence to counter any negative situation with compassion. Anger has been absent and shows no sign of returning.

Our beliefs define who we are, and betraying them can lead us down a path of confusion and uncertainty. Staying true to our beliefs will always keep us in control of our lives. It is possible to achieve freedom from the enslavement of our sins. Change will only come when we wholeheartedly believe in the outcome.

CHAPTER FOURTEEN

THIS JOURNEY HAS NO END

FINDING PURPOSE IN LIFE AND
THE COURAGE TO PURSUE IT

*"I put all my trust in God; everything else will
come naturally. Eventually, it will fall into
place. I found my true purpose in life: faith."*

I HAVE SPENT THE FIRST half of my life seeking the essence
of living and will spend the second half learning how to
die. I will die without shame and aim to depart righteously.

My forty-first year on Earth in 2023 has been one of
my worst yet most blissful. I would not change a thing;
every series of events has brought me to this moment. The
struggle was a blessing. The thought of how insignificant
we are and that I would never make a difference or change
this world averted my desire to seek the true purpose of
my life. I now have discernment and an understanding
of what I am experiencing and why it is happening. I am
grateful for creation.

Finally, my time has been productively utilized in writing
this manuscript. Whether the book is a success does not
matter. Selling one or a thousand copies would be equally
perfect. The process and completion of the book would be
a success in and of itself.

With the manuscript nearing its completion, the feeling
is indescribable. The unimaginable idea has manifested into

reality. Someone who constantly thought less of himself—self-pity, without talent, an average person working six days a week, content with life, and less virtuous—could complete an inconceivable task.

Have you ever thought of an idea that was supposed to be impossible to achieve that you did not accomplish? Uncover the motivation to self-improve. Discover the joy in educating and improving yourself, even in things beyond your interest. Our minds, not outside sources, create happiness. Embrace your life, creativity, and ideas.

As we come to the closing chapter of this book, we may wonder why the words "negative energy" and "positive energy" are used so frequently throughout the book—the method of identifying what is good and what is bad. Identifying negative and positive thoughts helps make sound judgments and decisions. Positive and negative energy is my interpretation of good as Christ and evil as the D. To live with a balance of both—to embrace the good and the bad.

Beyond doubt, I have experienced a glimpse of what I thought heaven would be like: no worries, no stress, and full of love and positivity. At age forty-two, I decided to be water baptized with my son, Max, at Word of Life Church. I now acknowledge that life encompasses more than having a job and providing for yourself and one's family. I yearn to live for others and am not afraid to do anything. Feeling untouchable from the evil spirit, faith in myself, and passion for self-progress have added potency to the courage and the will to accomplish the unthinkable. I am motivated with strength, hope, and faith.

We can take substantial steps toward self-improvement before a low point or hardship. Rather than being reactive, we can choose to be proactive by seeking motivation to inspire us to make changes immediately, without delay. Find the passion for hungering for a better life, educating and challenging yourself, and becoming a better person. The ideas are within your reach.

Countless people are on their journey to finding truth, love, forgiveness, and positivity. However, this world is full of evil spirits and wrongdoers who try to suppress these stories and experiences, which can be remarkable and influential sources of information. I understand that our lives can influence others around us, and therefore, I am not living just for me but for my children and future generations.

Coming to faith has resulted in the manifestation of this book, inspired by the intention of sharing mindful experiences and transformation. Faith will share my journey and guide this message to reach those with and without faith.

The confession of my shame allowed me to break free from its grasp. I no longer live by shame, and it will no longer be inherited with future choices and actions. As I continue to live a life of truth, I have faith that others will one day open their hearts, as I did, and share their spiritual journeys.

We are not perfect; that is a fact. But we are freed from the powers of sin. We have a choice to live a life free of sin, free of the evil influence. And we all can strive to live the remainder of our lives perfectly, as our paths to righteousness have been laid before us.

What is wrong with that? Why have we become so afraid to desire perfection? Can we achieve perfection?

We know we are not and cannot be perfect, but this notion prevents us from striving for perfection. We have allowed sin to seize our lives willingly, and in modern times it has become challenging to identify what constitutes a sin. Due to the prevalence and normality of sin, our way of life has isolated and hindered the path to living well.

Be unique by striving for a perfect life. Even with limited resources, achieving a high-quality life at any stage is possible. Success should be sought in all areas, not just financial stability. A well-rounded person should focus on their relationships, health, and spiritual and mental well-being. We all face inner demons throughout our lives, but it's never too late to summon the courage to conquer our fears and start anew. We can all strive toward a peaceful and perfect life.

Continuous change has set a path to control our thinking, emotions, speech, and mindset, which means we are suited to change. We have the tools and means to recondition ourselves to enjoy everything: music, food, hobbies, interests, and even people. We all know or at least have an idea of the answers to our lives. The question is, Are we courageous enough to choose that path?

The beauty of our journey is that we are capable of anything: the courage to write a book, even if you have never read one or are not the reading type; the courage to coach; the courage to be social and attain meaningful friendships; the courage to overcome the fears of change; the courage to overcome our comfort zones—to go beyond boundaries. Find the courage to ask for forgiveness. Acknowledging and admitting faults is crucial and should never be given up on. Never give in. Positively facing calamity and unfortunate events can help you earn a smile every day, turning bad days into good ones. Creating meaningful, long-lasting relationships is vital as you embark on your journey.

Confess and forgive yourself for past sins and those who have sinned against you. Do not harbor hate for those who have done you harm, as it can destroy your spirit. Sin no more. Judge no more. Struggle less with your convictions. Live a life of absolute truth, compassion, and empathy. Stay on the path to perfection—the path toward inner peace.

Forgive one another and view each other with love and positivity. Be truthful and honest, and always self-reflect on ways to improve. We can fix ourselves one hundred percent.

We can share our stories and experiences with patience. Our mindful silence through our acts and behavior is the balance of our words—equally powerful and influential. Let us grow together on this ongoing quest for truth, forgiveness, and a splash of optimism. Keep progressing and live the rest of your life well. The path to heaven awaits on Earth and after.

Your journey, your path to truth,
forgiveness, and positivity.

I AM GRATEFUL

MY LOVING WIFE WAS sent to help me find the courage to live meaningfully, uncover my potential, and unveil my faith. Without my wife's unconditional faith and unquestionable support from the beginning, this manuscript would not be truthful in its entirety. This would never have happened if my wife had the slightest doubt about proceeding with the manuscript. The idea to pen this manuscript would not have come to fruition if I had not been genuinely truthful to her, myself, and others. Her sacrifice was shown throughout this process, while enduring my endless lectures and words. I wholeheartedly appreciate and thank you, my dear. To my boys, Max and Micah, I live for you.

Then there is the greatest man in my life—my stepfather, Frank—the essence of a gentleman. He has been a pillar of strength in my life. Without him, it would have taken a different direction. This memoir is a testament to his guidance, discipline, and profound impact on my life.

To my late mother-in-law: I treasured our time together. Your whisper was heard, and my prayers were answered. I am blessed to have known you. Thank you for watching over us.

Without my sister, Nina, I would be lost. Her encouragement and positivity are unmatched, and they help me through the tough times. I am genuinely thankful for our many lengthy conversations, which contributed significantly to the development of this story.

Much of the credit for this book goes to Pastor Joel, for whom I am humbly grateful for his existence, presence, faith, and words. His words saved my life. *The Courage to Live a Meaningful Life* could not have been completed without his blessings. Pastor Joel and Word of Life Church are the foundation of my faith—the foundation of this manuscript.

With gratitude, Jonathan's role is quite special. He is not only a brother-in-law but a mentor and an inspiration. This memoir found its purpose with his insight, wisdom, and encouraging words. Along with helping with the title, Jonathan's influence can also be sensed throughout this book.

The proximity of Pastor Jennifer and Mrs. Dorothy (Momma Dot) was overlooked for years; their presence was finally felt and appreciated. God sent Mrs. Jennifer to watch over me through the years.

I am deeply grateful for Haley's prayers. Her faith has not only deepened our friendship but played a crucial role in the initial development of this memoir. I am truly blessed to have her and her husband, Michael, in my life and I'm humbled by their devotion to God.

I would like to extend a special thanks and express my eternal gratitude to my editor, Matthew O'Brien. Our paths crossed by fate; this book was meant to be in Matthew's masterful hands. Without his unique guidance, unparalleled skill, and honest critiques, *The Courage to Live a Meaningful Life* would never have achieved its full potential—it would just be another book. Editors sometimes get a bad name, but it was a joyful experience and encouraging to encounter a genuine stranger who was passionate about his craft and about helping others with theirs.

Last but certainly not least, I am thankful for my family, extended family, and friends: Sara, Cindy, and Angela, as well as my three sisters-in-law, Elizabeth, Selina, and Jessica. Without you, there is no me and there is no book. I am grateful for your love and support, especially for adapting to my changes and lectures. This book is for you.